An old Indian approached and asked for some food. Delbert Penrod went over the campfire to dish some up when he sensed movement behind him. He turned in time to see the Indian reaching for his six-shooter....

While John hauled freight, Cynthia feared for her life living far from her nearest neighbors. News spread that a man murdered a husband and wife by cutting their throats. One night, while Cynthia and her children were in the kitchen, she looked out the window and the murderer stared back at her. Cynthia screamed....

Jake, his wife and two children, along with a neighbor child, became stranded in their freezing car in one of the worst blizzards ever to hit the White Mountains. Jake got out of the car and started to walk the many miles to town on the deserted road. Blanche stayed in the car and kept the children awake for two days...She pinched, slapped and even resorted to setting their hair on fire then quickly slapping it out....

TOP O' THE PINES

Life in Pinetop and the White Mountains

by
Gene Luptak

Gene Luptak

Ponderosa Pine Press   Pinetop, Arizona

Copyright © 2004 by Gene Luptak

All rights reserved. No part of this book may be reproduced or transmitted in any form or by any means, electronic or mechanical, including photocopying, recording, or by any information storage and retrieval system, without permission in writing from the author.

This edition was prepared for printing by
Ghost River Images
5350 East Fourth Street
Tucson, Arizona 85711
www.ghostriverimages.com

In memory of my parents,
Martin and Jeannette Luptak,
who first took me to the White Mountains.

Front Cover: Woodland Lake in Pinetop.
Photo by Dawn Luptak.
Back Cover: Rodeo-Chediski Fire comes dangerously close to Show Low and Pinetop-Lakeside.
Photo by Laura L. Haney. Used by permission.

ISBN 0-9759005-0-1

Library of Congress Control Number: 2004095912

Printed in the United States of America
Second Printing: September, 2004
10 9 8 7 6 5 4 3 2 1

Contents

Introduction vi

Mountain Meadow 1
Neighbors Arrive 7
Pinetop's Real McCoy 19
Corydon E. Cooley 25
Love at First Sight 33
Abe Amos & Friends 39
Living Among Apaches 43
Jake Renfro 55
Charlie Clark's 59
Walsh Mack 71
Lakeside 77
McNary 89
Schools 93
The Mountain Lights Up 99
Pinetop on the Move 109
The Two Shall Become One 117
Pinetop People 125
Evacuation 139
Sweep Across the Mountain 159

Bibliography 169
Author's Notes and Acknowledgments 171
Index 175
About the Author 190

Introduction

Several centuries ago, perhaps about the time Columbus reached the Americas, a tiny Western Yellow Pine seedling poked its head out of the ground and stretched skyward.

Years went by and this Ponderosa seedling grew into a slender tree with a few sparse branches stretching from its trunk. A bear sauntered by, brushing its side against a branch. Off in the distance an elk bugled its male challenge.

Many more years went by and the skinny tree now stood ram-rod straight, 90 feet tall with strong branches stretching into a green canopy. A creek flowed nearby and fish splashed through the water. They were on alert to hide from enemies such as bears, raccoons and wolves. The creek someday would be called "Billy Creek," and biologists would name the fish "Apache trout." But that was still centuries away.

Long before the tree sprouted and started to push upward, Indians had roamed this area that eventually would be called the White Mountains of Arizona. They were here, perhaps, as far back as 18,000 years ago. These Archaic Culture people hunted, gathered plant food and lived in pit houses, disappearing about 5,000 years ago.

Next came Mogollon prehistoric peoples who slowly evolved from Archaic hunter-gathers into farmers and village-dwellers.

The most telltale Mogollon undertaking in this area began about 1250 A.D. on a rim of volcanic rock near Springerville. It's called *Casa Malpais*.

This "House of the Badlands" probably served as a special religious place. Ceramic bowls are found in rooms obviously used as meeting halls. More people could gather in a large, square kiva. Beneath the rooms, in a series of natural caverns, the Indians built stone walls and roofs for their sealed burial crypts.

But, the Mogollon also disappeared. The ancestors of the Apache and Navajo Indians drifted down from Alaska and Canada and moved into the area. A pueblo that was abandoned in the 14th Century has been unearthed in the center of Show Low. Apaches eventually evolved and separated themselves from their northern Navajo cousins. Other tribes in the West didn't like them. The Zuni called them "Apachu," meaning "the enemy." The Apaches in general were warlike, but the Apache clans that settled in the White Mountains were more peaceful. Instead of raiding other Indians and settlers, they became more involved with raising crops such as corn and squash.

The first non-Indians believed to come to the White Mountains were Francisco Vasquez de Coronado and his large army of men. They were looking for the Seven Cities of Gold.

They left Mexico City on Feb. 23, 1540, and many days later camped for two days at the Black River crossing south of present-day Whiteriver. They traveled along the west side of the north fork of the White River and passed by the area that is now McNary. They camped near Lake Mountain Lookout Tower, where several of Coronado's soldiers ate poison hemlock and died. Coronado said he saw neither Apaches (although they were in the area) nor gold.

Early in the 1800s, fur trappers appeared on the Mountain, but the beavers were not to their liking and the trappers left. Early Spanish settlers named the White Mountains (*Sierra Blanca*) because in those days the mountain tops wore a crown of snow almost half the year. Then later in the century came the sheepmen, cattlemen, farmers, outlaws, cavalry, lumbermen and Mormon colonists to the White Mountains.

One of the colonists was Joseph Peterson, who settled in Lakeside in 1906. His daughter, Leora Peterson Schuck, remembers what the forest looked like in 1907:

"Straight clean trunks reaching 25, 30 or 40 feet before branches started, only a few small pines. Here and there clumps of oak, but surprisingly little underbrush. One could see several hundred yards through the trunks of the trees. It was 10 or 15 years later, after countless mature trees had been sawed down for lumber, that the small ones began growing in jungle-like proportions, and the old vistas were gone. It will never be like that again."

And the tree along the creek that sprouted in Columbus' time? It is now more than 175 feet high and more than 400 years old. It's once dark-brown, rough bark is now a smoother yellowish-brown—the mark of a mature Ponderosa pine. Unfortunately, this old tree that is eight-feet in diameter in the early 1900s is now a prime target for the men who will build sawmills along Billy Creek.

Mountain Meadow

John William Phipps traveled on a rutted wagon trail that weaved through the forest of the Mogollon Rim mountain range. Descending from a mountainside summit, he rode into a huge meadow. Nearby a spring bubbled up. Other streams cascaded from the nearby foothills and flowed through the meadow. No need to travel on; Phipps found what he was looking for. On April 18, 1885, Phipps dismounted and began making plans to stake out his homestead in this fertile valley. Pinetop had its first resident. His nearest neighbor most likely lived several miles away.

Phipps, a bachelor, had many reasons to settle in this meadow. Just beyond the distant trees lay the Fort Apache Indian Reservation, home of the White Mountain Apache Tribe. Alcoholic beverages could not be legally sold on the reservation and soldiers from Fort Apache had to travel off Indian lands to buy booze. Phipps' hideaway was as close as it could be, handy for the soldiers to buy drinks. Phipps built his saloon/home in which he also stocked general merchandise for the soldiers, Indians and anyone else who wandered through the area. More and more freighters were hauling goods in wagons from Holbrook to Fort Apache. They usually came by Phipps' place because it was the easiest way to get over the nearby summit. When not tending bar, Phipps hitched up horses to his wagon and made extra money hauling freight to Fort Apache and elsewhere. He also farmed about 15 acres in this fertile meadow.

In 1886 or 1887, depending on what report you believe, the William Lewis Penrod family moved from their home in Show Low to Phipps' meadow. They lived in their wagon box for 10 days while William and his son, Ralph, cut logs and built a one-room cabin. When interviewed in 1950, Ralph Penrod told writer-photographer Norman Mead that his family could see smoke from the cabin of their only neighbor, Johnny Phipps.

Phipps and the Penrods co-existed. Some of William Penrod's married children moved to the meadow to be next to Mom and Dad. The population of "Pinetop" grew from one in 1885 to close to 50 in just a few years. Most of them were Penrods.

At first, the area was called Penrodville, or Penrod, although William Penrod was reported not too keen to have the settlement named after him. Besides, it is reported, the U.S. Post Office already had another Penrod someplace else and it wasn't pleased with the idea either.

White Mountains' historian Richard Lynch, a University of Arizona professor, contends the second name of the Phipps-Penrod community was called *"Mal Pai."* A Mal Pai post office opened on June 7, 1890. John W. Phipps became the postmaster, according to "Arizona Territory Post Offices & Postmasters." (*Mal Pai*, Spanish for "bad land," referred to the ubiquitous malapai volcano rock in the area.)

Lynch said the Mormons in the area objected that saloon-keeper Phipps ran the settlement's post office, and that's why they applied pressure on postal authorities to dissolve the post office. They succeeded and Phipps' postmaster tasks ended less than two months later on Aug. 4, 1890. However, on Dec. 9, 1891, Edward E. Bradshaw was named postmaster of the new "Pinetop" post office.

How did residents settle on the "Pinetop" name? There are a couple theories. Since the Fort Apache soldiers had to climb a mountain to get their booze, they reportedly told each other, "Let's go to the top of the pines" or "Let's go get high (drunk) at the top of the pines." Eventually they cut the verbiage and just called the place Pinetop.

Ralph Penrod disagreed. He contended the settlement was named after Walt Rigney's head. Rigney ran Phipps' store and saloon and the soldiers called him Pinetop. Penrod, in an article in the 2000 *Arizona White Mountains* magazine, was quoted: "...because of the pointed shape of his (Rigney's) head and the unusual hair style he wore...his head looked like a pine tree." Mead, who had interviewed Ralph Penrod, said Penrod was dead serious about the truth of this story.

Regardless of which story is correct, two things appear to be certain: the soldiers named the place Pinetop and William L. Penrod and his family approved the name.

The growing number of settlers had more important things on their minds than naming the town and engaging in post office squabbles. During the late 1880s and early 1890s, Phipps, the Penrods and other newcomers to the area had to make a living. They cleared the land, hauled off rocks, cut trees and planted crops. They enlarged the original ditch constructed by Phipps to bring water to their land. This caused problems for Henry Huning, a Show Low farmer.

On June 19, 1894, Huning filed a complaint against Phipps, William Penrod and others declaring that these men diverted water from Show Low Creek, diminishing his prior appropriation.

In his complaint, Huning asserted both Phipps and Penrod constructed a dam on the center fork (Billy Creek) of Show Low Creek, according to Salt River Project's

Shelly C. Dudley who wrote a report in 1994 of the history of water development in the White Mountains.

The Pinetop residents, along with settlers in the tiny Woodland community about three miles away, responded to the lawsuit.

"Phipps and Penrod declared they had been on the east of Center Fork...for more that five years prior to the suit (and) they claimed to have appropriated and used water for the continuous irrigation of 25 acres of land," said Dudley.

Other residents of the Pinetop-Woodland area that later were named in the original lawsuit were Edward Bradshaw, Charles Savage, John Hall, Bill Stephens, Hans Hansen, Nephi Packer and additional members of the Penrod family. They all stated they had been using the waters for many years prior to the filing of the litigation.

"In dry periods, the (Pinetop/Woodland residents) claimed to have used all the waters of the fork of Show Low Creek for irrigation and domestic uses and if this water supply was denied their use, they would have to leave the settlement.

"...Huning attested that at different times prior to 1894, when he had a low flow in the creek, he notified certain of the defendants, including Penrod and Phipps, and shortly after his water supply would increase.

"Phipps (who was irrigating 15 acres) acknowledged that the Penrods, without his objection or authority, enlarged the ditch while knowing Huning had a right to the waters of Show Low."

The trial began on Dec. 4, 1895 before the District Court of the Fourth Judicial District for Navajo County. The judge divided up the water to all parties. He allowed the Pinetop and Woodland farmers to have enough water to irrigate 37 acres and "that all parties be enjoined from interfering with them."

Needless to say, Huning wasn't exactly thrilled with the decision allowing Phipps and others to siphon off water reaching his Show Low farm.

Also, according to Dudley, Phipps filed a claim for 160 acres of unsurveyed lands on July 19, 1893, asserting a settlement date of April 18, 1885. The claim for lands was located in Township 8 North, Range 23 East in the northeast corner of Section 5. This would be in the area south of where the Pasta House restaurant and the Nine Pines Motel are located today. State Route 260 probably runs through what was once Phipps' property.

This lawsuit and homestead claim in the mid1890s is the last time Phipps' name was recorded in any legal document. Very little has been written about him; his name pops up now and then in various diaries and reports written primarily by the town's early settlers.

Phipps "life is shrouded in mystery," according to Leora Peterson Schuck, who wrote about the Penrods. "Research by interested residents has failed to turn up any information as to his origin, how long he remained in the country, or where he went."

Recent discoveries show that John W. Phipps was born in 1838 in Virginia. He later was a resident of Fort Apache, according to the 1880 and 1882 U. S. Census rolls. It is believed he was a soldier there.

It is not known when Phipps died or where his grave is located. Legend has it he was buried near a (a) peach tree (b) apple tree or (c) willow trees near Nine Pines Motel. No gravestone or headboard with his name on it has been found, although there is a fenced-off gravesite outlined with stones south of the motel. Locals claim that plot houses Phipps' remains. Years ago, Sue Penrod and her Girl Scouts fenced in the gravesite and outlined the alleged grave with stones.

However, according to official records at the state capital in Phoenix, there apparently was another "John W. Phipps" in Arizona. He died April 16, 1916 in Prescott. A few days later a one-paragraph obituary on this Phipps appeared in Prescott's newspaper. He was 69 years old when he died; he was a miner and the owner of properties in the Kirkland (near Prescott) area. His remains were sent to relatives in Pennsylvania. Apparently, this Phipps was a miner in Colorado about the same time Pinetop's Phipps farmed and served drinks. Thus, Prescott's Phipps had relatives and recorded history about him. Pinetop's Phipps, as far as anyone can determine, didn't have any known relatives and nobody apparently bothered to write anything about his background.

Thus, the origin of Pinetop is this: the certain whereabouts of the remains of the town's founder is suspected, but not proven; the settlement once was named after a porous rock; and there is a possibility that Pinetop was named after a man's pointy head which looked like a tree.

Neighbors Arrive

The smoke from Johnny Phipps' chimney wafted across the meadow, greeting Pinetop's second resident, William Lewis Penrod, along with his wife Polly Ann and their brood of nine sons and daughters.

Penrod, who was then in his mid-50s, built his log cabin in 1887 in Phipps' meadow. His daughter-in-law, Annie Penrod, said in her account of William Penrod that Phipps welcomed the family.

William Penrod was born Jan. 27, 1832 in Union County, Ill., and moved to Utah in 1849 with his family. There, he met and married Polly Ann Young, who had crossed the plains by ox team from Tennessee. The couple had 12 children while living in Utah.

On Oct. 26, 1878, William and Polly Ann Penrod, along with nine children, left Utah for Arizona. (Two children, Mary Ann and David, had already married, and a third child, Heber, 12, was killed in a hay-mowing accident in 1872 while lying in an alfalfa field.) The family was heeding a call to help colonize a wilderness area in Arizona for the Church of Jesus Christ of Latter-day Saints.

The Penrods arrived in the White Mountains at Show Low on Dec. 31, 1878 and camped in an old house belonging to a sheepherder. That summer, they moved onto John Willis' ranch and looked after the rancher's cattle. Daughter Temperence Susan, 18, married William Stephens at the Willis ranch on Sept. 25, 1879.

Penrod later moved his family to Juniper (Linden) where he tried his hand at dry farming. A rumor spread that the Apaches would begin an uprising and all the farmers and ranchers in the area fled to Corydon E. Cooley's ranch at Show Low. Cooley, who had lived in the area for a number of years, had married two daughters of Apache Chief Pedro.

One of Penrod's sons, Liona, later wrote: "If it hadn't been for Mr. Cooley, I guess we would have been massacred."

Cooley and William Penrod became friends and two of Penrod's sons, Albert and Delbert, went to work for Cooley in the fall of 1880. Meanwhile, William Penrod went into business making wooden shingles for settlers' homes.

The following year, Polly Ann Penrod gave birth to their 13th child, Geneva. In 1883, William Penrod, with Polly Ann and their younger children, moved back to Utah, only to return to the White Mountains almost three years later. Meanwhile, sons David, Albert and Delbert stayed behind and hauled freight from Wilcox to Globe. Mary Ann, a widow, and Ephraim also stayed behind and looked after the family farm.

When William returned from Utah after failing at dry farming there, he and David set out from Show Low in 1886 or 1887 to find a place with plenty of water to raise crops. That's when they discovered, 15 miles away, the beautiful Pinetop meadow with water running through it. William Penrod and son Ralph built a one-room log cabin in 10 days. In the spring of 1888, they cut trees and planted crops. William built another shingle mill, and later constructed a six-room house. His older children eventually moved to Pinetop to be near their parents. In fact, all

Freighters hauling goods in wagons
near Willcox. Circa: 1907.
Arizona Historical Society AHS# 48677

12 of their children plus numerous grandchildren lived in Pinetop at the same time. (In the 1910 U.S. Census, 55 of the 95 people living in Pinetop belonged to the Penrod clan)

When the Penrods first arrived in Pinetop, the men could only find work shearing sheep for William Amos. Once, while the men were away, daughter Mary began preparations to wash clothes when two Indian men rode into the yard.

"They had fish to sell," according to history on a Penrod website. "When we wouldn't buy them, one of them took off his dirty handkerchief and made Mary wash it, then he tried to get her to go with him and live. She grabbed her baby and ran over to (David's) place. The

Indians thought this great sport and how they did laugh. They followed her over there. Dave's wife, Cynthia Ann, knew how to handle Indians and soon got rid of them."

Later, the Penrods built a sawmill in Pinetop. They continued to farm their land. "They were a thrifty family and always lived within their means, never going in debt or mortgaging their home," according to the website.

This family and other Pinetop residents loved to dance. Ralph owned and operated a dancehall for 16 years. He also played fiddle at dances in Pinetop and surrounding communities. Sometimes the entire family would drive as far as 25 miles to attend a dance. William was known as "Whistling Bill," because he whistled morning, noon and night. "We all knew Father was coming; the whistle got there before he did," son Liona said.

The Penrod's youngest child, Geneva, married George Hall in Pinetop on Dec. 24, 1900. That left only Ralph at home with Mom and Dad. At age 30, Ralph went to Greer to visit his brother, David, who was a forest ranger at the time. There, Ralph met Sarah Ann Butler, and they began courting. On July 17, 1905, they married at the Greer home of the bride's father, Jacob N. Butler.

For the first time, William and Polly Ann were alone in their six-room house. "They were always open to welcome their children back, but they (children) were never allowed to smoke in the house; they were asked to step outside to smoke," according to information on the Penrod website.

Polly Ann had been frail for many years and on April 9, 1909, she died. William Penrod died seven years later at age 84. Both are buried in the Penrod plot at the old Pinetop cemetery located at the end of Penrod Lane. Someone, in 1942, counted William and Polly Ann Penrod's descendants. The total was 897. It is hard to estimate what that number would be today.

• • •

William Penrod

    The desperados jumped in front of the covered wagon on the road between Clifton and Pinetop. Inside were Ephraim Penrod, his wife and children. With guns drawn, the badmen asked for the Penrod's horses and money. During the stand-off, son Elmer popped his head out between the wagon flaps and said, "Howdy Floyd." Elmer had gone to school with Floyd, the son of one of the would-be crooks. The robbers begged Eph not to tell the sheriff, offering them almost anything in exchange for their silence. The robbers left empty-handed and the Penrods continued on their way home to Pinetop.

• • •

Among the many jobs Delbert Penrod had devised to earn money was hauling freight for the U.S. government between Holbrook and Fort Apache. On one of those trips, he stopped at noon to eat and to feed and water his eight-horse team.

An old Indian approached and asked for some food. Delbert bent over the campfire to dish up some when he sensed movement behind him. He turned in time to see the Indian reaching for his six-shooter that was buried in his holster. Del leaped across the fire and whipped the gun out, aiming it at the Apache, who immediately fell on his knees, pleading for his life. "Get out o' here!" Del threatened. The Indian hastily crawled and then ran away. The wagon's provisions and eight horses would have been a nice haul for the Indian.

• • •

In 1892, Mormon officials decided to hold an Arizona all-stake convention in Pinetop. About 1,100 Mormons from throughout the state—many from the Salt River Valley, Safford, and St. John's, as well as White Mountains Mormon strongholds such as Snowflake, Taylor and Show Low area—attended over the July 4th weekend. Four LDS elders from Salt Lake City also traveled to Pinetop by train and horse and buggy for the conference.

The Penrods and other Pinetop and Woodland Mormons built a 2,400-square-foot dance pavilion for the event. The Salt Lake City delegation warned that only square dancing would be allowed, not the more worldly "round" dancing. After the Utah visitors left, the Arizona Mormons disobeyed and they round danced. (The pavilion was used for special occasions until it burned in the 1920s)

• • •

"When the Penrods first came to Pinetop," said Martin Penrod, grandson of patriarch William Penrod, "the only jobs available were shearing sheep, for which they were paid three cents per sheep."

Liola Penrod and his twin brother, Liona, were known as the best sheep shearers in the area. They each could shear 100 sheep in one day. There was no electricity; they had to use hand shears.

• • •

In those early days, the Penrods had to drive a team and wagon about 130 miles to Gallup, New Mexico, for supplies and groceries. It took days for the trip. Later, as Holbrook developed into a town, they drove there for their shopping. Travel time was cut in half.

• • •

In 1898, the Penrods built a 25-by-50-foot dance hall in Pinetop. At one end was a huge heating stove that could burn four-foot-long logs.

As the Pinetop settlers faced the beginning of a new century, the residents decided to throw a big New Year Eve's bash on Dec. 31, 1899. The Fort Apache post band performed and people from throughout the area arrived and danced all night to welcome in the 1900s.

• • •

Joe Mettie of Lakeside remembers the time when three different Penrods owned three separate grocery stores in Pinetop.

• • •

Martin Penrod remembered the times his friends and he would swim at Rocky Pond in Pinetop. "It (the pond) had a V-shape lined with rocks and we'd build a fire then go swimming," Martin said. "One time Clem Adair threw some .22 shells into the fire and we were all standing naked around the fire; boy did we scatter when those (bullets) went off. Arch Penrod was laughing like hell and took off running when one shell hit him in the rear end."

Martin, born in 1903 to Albert and Mary Penrod, lived in Pinetop until about 1916, when his family moved and started a ranch in Pinyeon, about 10 miles northeast of Pinetop. He died in 1997. Here are some of his recollections as recorded by Merry Penrod and Adele Twomey:

- "...Dad ran the...saloon in Pinetop. At the time I first started school there were only 15 families in Pinetop. There was only one store owned by (Sylvester) McCoy. The post office was run by my Aunt Seid Penrod, Uncle Dell's wife.

- "...For entertainment on Saturdays and Sundays, we'd go out on Blue Ridge and round up wild burros on foot and run them. In those days we didn't have any horses.

- "...Years ago when anyone died (before there were mortuaries) they'd put the body by an open window and pack ice around them until they got the coffin made and ready to bury them. I can remember Arve and I sitting with Grandpa Penrod's body; this was at Aunt Susie Stevens house. Louie...made the most beautiful coffins I'd ever seen. You furnished the timber and supplies and he'd stay up all night making them. You gave him a bottle of whiskey, that's all the pay he'd ever take. Ma always wanted him to make her coffin. However, he drowned long before she passed away.

- "...When I was a kid I decided I wanted a violin, so I went door-to-door selling bluing (a substance to whiten clothes). Finally, I made enough to buy my violin. I messed around for several days trying to learn to play and didn't so I threw the damn thing away. My brother, George, picked it up and in a few days was playing tunes."

- (Martin produced an old ledger for 1905-06 from the Babbitt's store in Holbrook where his father, Albert, shopped. Prices included a pair of overalls for 85 cents; pair of boots for $4.75; pound of coffee for 19 cents; flannel cloth for 12 1/2 cents per yard; a pound of bacon for 12 1/2 cents; chocolate for 25 cents a pound; a dozen eggs for 25 cents, and 100 pounds of flour for $4.)

- ".. I can remember when we were kids and there were six of us boys. Ma was a very small woman, but she was loud. We all had to make our beds before going to breakfast. Ma would always inspect them to see if they were properly made. If they weren't, the bedding was dumped on the floor and you re-made the bed until it was right, or no breakfast.

- "...When Ret and Bell left home to get married, this left the housework to George and me. Mostly, we had to scrub clothes for Mom on a scrub board. Many a time our knuckles were sore and bleeding. Dad finally got a wooden washer that had a wheel on top with a handle to pull back and forth.

- "...In 1918 the snow was very deep. It came to the top of the fence posts after Dad drove a sled back and forth to pack it down. We made a V-drag hitched to a team of horses and drug the roads to each family and then down to the lake. We then drove the cattle to the lake and cut the ice so that the cattle could (drink).

- "...When I was 17 years old we all loved to sleigh ride. Many a time we'd have two or three teams of horses hitched to our sleigh and ride all over Lakeside, Pinetop and McNary. Sometimes we'd ride until 12 or one o'clock at night.

- "...I remember a little black-haired gal always chasing me. She was married, too. I remember she went to California and when she returned her husband asked if I'd drive the team and wagon he'd borrow to McNary to pick her up. He was really a nice guy so I said "sure." His wife climbed into the seat between us and she put her arm around me and into my pocket. God, was I scared I'd get shot. We (Martin and her husband) were both carrying guns, too. I just ignored her and was relieved when I drove them home. Lord, did she ever chase after me.

- "...The Great Depression was very bad. If you didn't raise your own food you just didn't make it. I'd shell corn, several bushels usually, load it on the wagon and take it into town to trade for coffee, sugar, flour and any other items to be had. We all ate a lot of cornbread, beans, molasses and jackrabbits. There just wasn't work available, so, of course, no money to be had. To this day I detest cornbread and beans.

- "...During the Depression years you could borrow money from FHA for chickens and cattle. Wal and I both borrowed money and bought chickens. Within two weeks mine came down with roop and every damn one died. So ended my chicken ranching. Wal's did very well and each week he had at least 36 dozen eggs to take into town to sell. With what money I had left, I bought six cows and calves and did just fine.

- "...The medicines at that time were onions and sugar syrup for coughs; ground deer horns and garlic for worms... Ma was great at making us drink black pepper tea for colds or coughs. Many times us boys would wait until she went to bed then we'd make a toddy (whiskey), then wash the cup and sprinkle pepper in the bottom. I don't know if she was ever wise to us. Surely she was.

- "...George (my brother) and I used to try our darnest to rope antelope, and the harder we'd ride into them the faster those bastards would run.
- ...When we first moved to the ranch in Pineyon, Dad planted sugar cane. We'd then strip the cane and haul it by wagon to Hal Butler's to be made into molasses. Later, we built a molasses mill.
- "...Dad used to have me plant beans. At one point I got tired of planting beans so I dug a big hole and threw a bunch of beans in it (not thinking they'd come up)...when Dad saw that bunch of beans, he said, "What's the matter, were you tired of planting beans?"
- "...John Stewart was one of the bootleggers in my early years. He had his still in a canyon near Pineyon. He made some of the best bootleg whiskey and would stay in the late hours of night running it off. He always brought me a gallon and left it by the door. One time he was quite drunk and using foul language, so Den and I threw him to the ground and tied him up and left him there for quite some time. Boy, was he mad when we untied him.
- "...In the early 1940s, Jim Finney deputized me to help take a man to jail in Show Low. This man had killed someone around Springerville and was arrested in Walsh Mack's place. He was handcuffed and in the front seat. Finney had me ride in the back seat; he said if he makes a move bat him over the head with your gun. At the time there wasn't a jail in Pinetop/Lakeside."

Pinetop's Real McCoy

After John W. Phipps and his legendary pointy-headed sidekick, Walt Rigney, operated Pinetop's first saloon/store, Sylvester McCoy came upon the scene to take over the tiny settlement's lone mercantile business. He settled in the area in 1894, staying until about 1920. The 1900 U.S. Census listed McCoy as a merchant in Show Low, while 10 years later he lived in Pinetop and he recorded his occupation as a merchant and farmer.

He also hauled freight with an eight-yoke oxen team between Holbrook and Fort Apache. On one occasion, according to James R. Jennings, in his book, *The Freight Rolled*, McCoy and oxen came upon the Willis brothers, whose wagon was stuck in the mud. McCoy told the brothers to get their 12 horses that were hitched to the wagon out of the way. He would "pull the dang thing out" with his oxen. The oxen pulled and tugged, and the wagon crept from the mud hole to more solid ground.

Toward the end of his freight-hauling career, McCoy operated a six-oxen team. Jennings quotes Wesley Jones, who lived in the White Mountains around 1900:

"Old man McCoy was colorful, as was his motley-colored, six-ox team. It was a sight to see his outfit pull into

Snowflake—six pair of wide horns undulating in the sun seemed to span the width of the road. The tall, lean creatures appeared taller than horses, with no harness except a huge yoke across their necks.

"Old man McCoy, with his wide felt hat and his wide mustache, sat in dignity atop his load. (He held) a long whip with a buckskin snapper on the end. Control of the team was mainly by voice and by expletives that oxen understand. McCoy always traveled alone, not from social hauteur, but because his stock moved at a slower pace. He made longer noon stops and made camp earlier in the evening. On stretches of bad road in winter, when horse teams were stuck in the mud, the McCoy outfit passed them all.

"It was interesting to watch the old man when in the mud. With every ox leaning in the yoke, all muzzles near the ground, the old fellow jumped up and down along the chair between the oxen, shouting names, curses and expletives. The wheels moved, ever so slowly, but moved and soon would be on solid ground."

After time, hauling with oxen got to McCoy. He wanted a simpler lifestyle and wanted to operate a mercantile enterprise and farm. He sold all six of his oxen to Billy Willis, who would fatten the beasts and slaughter them for beef.

Jones continues:

"Six or eight boys my own age, about 12 years (old), always managed to be on hand when word was passed that an ox was to be slaughtered. We wanted to retrieve the bladder which, when blown up and tied, made an excellent football. These ox bladders were larger and tougher than the ordinary product.

"Old Spot was the last to go. The fattening process took longer for him because of his poor teeth. The time chosen was sunset, the cool of the day. He was led without protest to the tall hoist in Uncle Billy's barnyard. Here he seemed to appraise the situation rather sniffingly, I thought. He was turned around for a better position. Then it happened. Old Spot blinked his eyes. There sat Joe Ramsey on pile of logs with a .44 Winchester rifle pointed straight in his face.

"Instantly, Spot hoisted his tail, burst loose and was off in the field, with men and boys in hot pursuit. Joe Ramsey, gun in hand, jumped on a horse, bareback, and gave chase. But he couldn't get his horse through fences where Old Spot went, and he had to go the long way around.

"It was dark when a lone shot was heard. Word was passed that Spot was down. Sure enough, he was on his back in an irrigation ditch, his four feet in the air. A wagon, axes, saws, lanterns, men and boys cleaned up the mess before midnight.

McCoy's Store

George Hall's Pinetop store in early 1900s

"Somehow I had no heart for the whole business, exciting as it was. I never confessed it, but secretly, in my heart, I hoped and prayed that Old Spot would get free."

It was unlikely McCoy was on the scene to see Old Spot gunned down. More than likely, he was some 25 miles away, operating his tiny store in Pinetop.

McCoy's one-room building contained both dry goods and groceries, as well as housing the post office. (He became Pinetop's fourth postmaster on Feb. 20, 1904. Other postmasters before him were Edward E. Bradshaw, appointed Dec. 9, 1891; Martha S. Packer, June 5, 1896, and Marintha A. Penrod, Jan. 21, 1899)

McCoy's store catered not only to residents of Pinetop, but to people living in nearby settlements of Woodland and Lakeside.

On Aug. 23, 1906, McCoy applied for a homestead on five acres, alleging settlement there in 1894. However, William Penrod also filed an entry on this same piece of property, claiming a settlement date of 1887. The records indicate that neither man received a patent for that portion of land.

In 1912, McCoy received a homestead patent for 50 acres, where he cultivated 30 acres of hay, beans, corn, wheat, oats and potatoes. It is likely he sold some of his crops from his store.

Jennings, as a lad, remembers the time while freighting with his father that they stopped at McCoy's "little two-by-four general store."

Jennings' dad ordered a pound of bacon.

"Mr. Jennings, I don't have any," McCoy replied. "You know, every time I get bacon, it is gone the first day. I just can't keep any on hand, so I had to quit handling it."

From that statement, it is clear that McCoy was a better freighter than a businessman.

Corydon E. Cooley

Army Scout Corydon E. Cooley and his trapper friend Buckskin Pete heard rifle shots. They snaked through the trees and saw renegade Apaches shooting at a small cabin on a fork of the Little Colorado River.

Holed up inside were George Frizell, commonly called "Professor," and his teenaged nephew, Sam Price. According to Roscoe G. Willson, in his book *No Place for Angels*, Prof and Price in the late 1870s came through northern Arizona with a wagon train, bringing with them about 100 head of cattle. They found the spot they wanted and built a cabin and corral. They didn't know that above the creek, nearby, lived Buckskin Pete amidst a grove of alders and aspen.

One day, Prof rode up the canyon and saw Pete's cabin. He yelled, and Pete came out. The two spent hours getting acquainted, and as Prof left, Pete warned: "I was over toward Camp Apache the other day and Scout Cooley, an old-timer married to an Apache woman, told me there was talk of the Mimbres Apaches planning a raid through here to drive out the settlers. Better keep an eye open and if trouble develops run your cattle up the canyon, and you and Sam come and stay with me 'till it's over."

25

The following morning, Prof got up and opened the front door. An arrow sped through the air and knocked his hat off. He slammed the door and yelled for Sam to get the guns. Peering out portholes, they saw about 15 to 20 Indians sneaking towards them. They shot a couple of Indians and the warriors retreated. "The shooting soon slowed down, although both sides continued exchanging intermittent shots," Willson noted.

Some Indians with dry grass and sticks advanced, while their cohorts blasted away toward the portholes. Prof and Sam waited. They knew the Indians planned to burn them out.

Distant rifle shots rang out, and Prof peeked out and saw one Indian stumble and fall while the others were running for their horses.

The battle over, Cooley and Buckskin Pete greeted Prof and Sam.

"This friend of mine is C.E. Cooley who lives up this side of Camp Apache," Pete said. "He came to my place last night to tell me the Mimbres Apaches under Victorio were out on a raid, and we were on our way down to warn you when we heard the shooting…we shot fast and they must have thought we were quite a crowd."

Cooley noticed the empty corral; the Indians had run off Prof's horses.

"Well," said Cooley, "Pete will ride back with me and bring you a flock of ponies. Won't cost you nothing. I've got dozens of 'em running loose."

And that gesture of kindness was common for Cooley. His reputation for often providing shelter and food to stranger and friend alike is legendary; he was known as a generous man during the nearly 50 years he lived in the White Mountains.

Corydon Eliphalet Cooley was born in 1836 in Virginia and at age 20 came out West to find gold and adventure. He failed to find the former, but he had plenty of wild tales to tell. During the Civil War, he joined the Union

Corydon E. Cooley
Arizona Historical Society AHS# 26353

Army and fought against Confederate forces in New Mexico.

Cooley managed a hotel, worked for a store that outfitted miners and fur trappers, and in 1869 came to the White Mountains with other prospectors looking for gold.

Lillie, left, Belle and Cora Cooley, three daughters of Corydon E. Cooley.
Arizona Historical Society AHS# 59389

Although he came up empty-handed, Cooley became an army scout and built a cabin near Camp Apache (later called Fort Apache) in 1870. He cultivated a few acres of corn, which he sold to the garrison. Later, he raised cattle.

In 1871, Cooley married two of Apache Chief Pedro's daughters, Molly and Cora. Cora died during childbirth five years later. Their daughter, Lillie, survived. When grown up, she married Del Penrod, a grandson of William L. Penrod, of Pinetop. Molly bore Cooley five children.

Also in 1871, General George Crook and his party trailblazed a route from Fort Apache to Camp Verde. "Crook's Trail" followed the upper reaches of the Mogollon Rim. Today it is basically Rim Road, going through Pinetop, Lakeside, Show Low and west towards Heber and beyond. Johnny Phipps, 15 years later, settled about a mile north of Rim Road in a fertile valley.

"The road forked westward near the Rim, just below the future site of Pinetop, and passed through the scattered ranches that subsequently became Show Low," said Thomas R. McGuire in his book, *Mixed-Bloods, Apaches, and Cattle Barons*.

The following year, Maj. John Green of the U.S. Army sent Cooley and a companion to mark "Crook's Trail."

Cooley fell in love with the area near Show Low and in 1873 he moved his family including his two Indian wives, and settled near the upper reaches of Silver Creek. Marion Clark, a bachelor and former Cooley ranch hand, had settled there earlier. Cooley and Clark joined forces and farmed and raised stock. "Cooley soon gained a reputation as a gracious and entertaining host to travelers on Crook's Trail," said McGuire.

In 1876, the pair decided to dissolve the partnership by playing a game of cards. Legend notes that Cooley showed the winning low card—possibly the deuce of clubs—and Clark moved on. "Show Low" reportedly then became the name of this growing mountain settlement. One source, historian Marshall Trimble, said Clark settled on a creek where Pinetop would be located, but there is no record of this. He must have moved on when Phipps and the Penrods arrived there about a decade later.

In the 1870s, Mormon colonists began arriving in the Show Low area. Alfred Cluff and David Adams worked for Cooley on his ranch. In 1877, Cluff rented land from Cooley and began raising his own crops. With several other Mormon colonists, Cluff settled about 1 1/2 miles above Cooley's ranch on Show Low Creek. In about 1880,

Cluff sold his ranch to fellow church member Frank Ellsworth.

With the increase of Mormon settlers growing crops, they began selling their harvests to Fort Apache. This was cutting into Cooley's profit, because he also sold to the fort. Cooley complained to the Mormons, who related his remarks to the elders in Salt Lake City.

According to H.B. Wharfield in his biography on Cooley, Church leader Brigham Young wrote Cooley a stern letter of admonishment:

"I understand you are an influential man, and our people are colonizing Arizona. If you treat them right you will be blessed, but if you do not you will go down, become a pauper in the land and your family will disown you and you will die a miserable death." Cooley sought revenge. He knew that Mormons had formed a colony at Forestdale on the Fort Apache Indian Reservation, and he lobbied the government to remove them. In 1883, authorities ordered the Mormons to move out of Forestdale and settle elsewhere. Other than that one incident, Cooley apparently held no animosity toward Mormons. He allowed them to fort-up on his ranch and even hired them for work.

In 1879, Cooley won election as an Apache County supervisor. (It wasn't until 1895 that Navajo County was carved out of Apache County.) Federal officials appointed him a deputy U.S. marshal. In 1880, Cooley became Show Low's first postmaster. This meant he had clout among governmental officials.

In the early 1880s, Cooley entered a partnership with Henry Huning, a successful rancher from Los Lunas, New Mexico. Cooley built a large two-story house with four chimneys on a hilltop, which is now the site of the town's LDS church. Cooley homesteaded 160 acres, which today is most of downtown Show Low. He sold his holdings to Huning in 1889 for $10,000 cash.

A year earlier, Cooley moved from Show Low and settled on the Indian reservation at the headwaters of Corduroy Creek, about five miles south of present-day Pinetop. William Penrod and family, who had earlier worked for Cooley in Show Low, had already settled next to Johnny Phipps in Pinetop's fertile valley.

Penrod and his sons built much of Cooley's new home in an open meadow surrounded by tall pines. The ex-scout and Indian fighter built up a herd of cattle with the C-Dart brand.

Territorial Gov. Nathan Murphy appointed Cooley a notary public for Pinetop in 1892. Cooley's children attended the Pinetop school.

Cooley eventually became related to the Penrod family. Cooley's daughter, Lillie, married Delbert L. Penrod, a grandson of patriarch William Penrod.

Del and Lillie had two sons, Howard (born 1914) and Logan (born 1917). Del developed a small dairy herd on the Fort Apache Indian Reservation. Del (1885-1963) and Lillie (1876-1968) both are buried in the Fort Apache Cemetery.

Cooley spent the rest of his life at his ranch south of Pinetop. He barely survived a stroke in 1911, which paralyzed him. He died at his ranch March 19, 1917, and was buried with military honors in the Fort Apache cemetery. On his gravestone his claim to fame listed him as a first lieutenant with the New Mexico Cavalry during the Civil War. Molly, his Apache wife, died three years later.

It is said that one of the reasons the White Mountain Apache Tribe remained mostly quiet during the Apache wars was because of the peaceful influence of Cooley. He spoke Apache, married Apache, his children were half-Apache, and he showed respect to any Apache he met. He was just as friendly and helpful to any white man who came his way. Without doubt, Cooley has attained legendary status in the White Mountains.

Love at First Sight

John Washington Adair rode into Pinetop planning to spend only a night and leave the next morning. Someone caught his eye and he decided to stay. The next thing we know about him is in 1894, at age 20, he married 16-year-old Cynthia Jane Penrod, William Lewis Penrod's granddaughter.

The couple lived in Nevada for a few months, but moved back to the White Mountains and started a 90-acre ranch about four miles southwest of Pinetop on the old road to Lakeside. They raised cattle, pigs and chickens.

John worked away from home most of the time hauling freight on horse-driven wagons between Fort Apache and Holbrook, as did many men living in the area in the 1890s.

While John hauled freight, Cynthia feared for her life, living far from her nearest neighbors. News spread that a man murdered a husband and his wife by cutting their throats. One night, while Cynthia and her children were in the kitchen, she looked out the window and the murderer stared back at her. Cynthia screamed, and the man disappeared. She stayed up all night holding a rifle.

John and Cynthia moved closer to town. They bought 75 acres south of where Charlie Clark's restaurant is now from Cynthia's father, David Israel Penrod. (Their house, which burned down in 1955, is now the site of Community Presbyterian Church on Pinetop's Penrod Lane.) The couple planted an apple orchard and a corn field, while John raised cattle and pigs. Electricity didn't come to their land until 1937. Family members through the years built their own houses on their parents' property.

During the flu epidemic of 1910, baby Thelma Gladys died and John buried her on property near the farm's southern border. His neighbors later asked if they could use the same area for burial of their loved ones. Thus, the Adair family says, John donated the land for Pinetop's pioneer cemetery. However, the Penrod family disagrees, contending that William Lewis Penrod owned the land and he donated the land for the Pinetop Cemetery.

For years, according to his grandson, Delbert Adair Jr., John and an Indian chief who both shared Feb. 10 as birthdays ran a foot race against each other. John became a Navajo County deputy sheriff and once tracked outlaws to Colorado.

On Sundays, the Adair family (the couple had 12 children) fixed a lunch and loaded up a buckboard and headed to Lakeside for church. They were active members of the Church of Jesus Christ of Latter-day Saints.

The family also made trips to attend parties and dances, sometimes traveling as far as Whiteriver for social events. Several of the Adair boys played instruments and often played at Saturday night dances in Pinetop and neighboring towns.

"John loved to whittle wood while visiting with family members," said Delbert Adair Jr. on the family's website. "He liked to dance and went to the local dance hall on Wednesday and Saturday nights. He wore elastic garter bands on his arms to hold his shirt sleeves up."

John Adair

However, John Adair faced many sorrows. He buried his wife and 11 of his 12 children. One son, John Robin Adair, who attended high school in Snowflake, was killed on summer vacation when a burning tree fell on him while fighting a forest fire.

Several of the family's favorite stories, some tragic, are recorded in the book *The John Washington Adair Family: Descendants included through 1998*.

"Dell (Delbert William, the seventh child, born in 1908) played the guitar and sang very well. He was scheduled to play and sing on the Joe Dana and Patsy Montano show on (Phoenix's) KOY Radio. Before the show, he was nervous and took a couple of drinks to calm himself down. Unfortunately, he had drunk a little too much and was unable to perform."

John's and Cynthia's fourth child, Clements, born in 1899, married the daughter of Nephi Packer and Mayzetta Penrod. He cut logs for a living. "Clem liked to wrestle and even required his future son-in-law, Louis Daniel, to wrestle him in order to marry his daughter, Virginia." Clem died at the Arizona State Hospital in Phoenix in 1951 while trying to overcome alcoholism, as did his brother, Leslie, a boxer, in the same year.

Lloyd Edwin, born in 1904, drowned in a creek near his parent's home in 1948.

Genevieve, born in 1918, was the 12th and last child born to John and Cynthia Adair. "She was spoiled rotten with all those brothers around, and she could never go anywhere without one or more of the boys escorting her. They all doted on her, including her mom and dad.

"Genevieve's first marriage was to Lloyd David Truscott...(they) met at The Blue Moon Dance Hall in Pinetop, and her brothers took delight in teasing her about Lloyd's height. He was just over 5-foot tall. When Lloyd came to pick Genevieve up for their first date, (tallest brother, Lloyd) opened the door. He stuck his head out and looked down the road one way, and then the other. He looked down at Lloyd David and asked him what his daddy sent him after. The family laughed about the incident for the rest of their lives."

On Oct. 10, 1951, John Adair's wife of 57 years died of cancer in Pinetop. Four years later, the 50-year-old home John built for his family, in which he lived, burned down. He lost everything he owned, including a pump organ and a large Bible with family records. For years, his wife kept a cedar chest in their bedroom. When someone gave her a gift such as a tablecloth or embroidered pillow case it would go into the chest unused. She even put hers and John's burial clothes in the cedar chest. Hers were used, but the fire destroyed John's.

After the devastating fire, John Adair moved in with his daughter, Genevieve, in Holbrook. She was the only child still alive. John died in 1957 at age 83.

On July 18, 1998, dozens of Adair descendants placed a monument in the Pinetop Cemetery in honor of John and Cynthia and the other family members buried there.

Abe Amos & Friends

Friends of Abe Amos remember the time when Pinetop scheduled a big party, but the town was out of liquor.

According to historian Tom McGuire, Abe, known as a friendly drinker, volunteered to ride horseback to Holbrook to buy some booze. Townspeople said he could not make it in only one day, but he did.

Amos had a gentler side. "Amos would also keep the youngsters of the Rim communities entertained," McGuire wrote. "He owned goats, and would hitch a pair to a toy wagon, pulling a load of delighted children through the streets."

Not much is known about Amos. One relative said he came to the Mountains from "the East," but another said he came from Oregon. What is known is that Abe, whose real name was Abraham Lincoln Amos, moved to the Pinetop area in the late 1880s or early 1890s with his parents and three brothers—Len, Will and C.D. (Dick).

Abe married Belle Crook Cooley, first child of Corydon E. Cooley and his Apache wife, Molly, in 1894. He and his brothers took up homesteads in the Pinetop-Woodland areas and what later would become Lakeside.

In the 1900 United States Census, Abe Amos (a "stockraiser") claimed Pinetop his home. Others living in Pinetop in 1900 were William Penrod (shingle maker), Merrill Willis (farmer), James Keith (day laborer), John Adair, Ephraim Penrod (day laborer), Nephi Packer, George Hall (day laborer), C. B. Stratton (sawmill worker) and John Heber Hansen (farmer).

Hansen, born in 1859, moved to Pinetop in August 1896, and hauled freight from Holbrook to Fort Apache. He also worked in a sawmill for John Colvin. In 1903 he moved to Show Low to farm. In the early 1900s he joined Niels Hansen (no relation) and others in buying land and colonizing Lakeside. At first, because five of the colonizers were Scandinavians, John Hansen called the new hamlet "Wooden Shoe." His friends overruled his suggestion and named it Lakeside.

Abe Amos and his brother Will raised sheep. Will lived in the area just west of present-day Rainbow Lake. It is believed that Abe moved there after 1900. In 1905, when the wool market collapsed, Abe and Will and other sheepmen of the area sold out to Mormons who were moving into the region.

Will sold his property to Niels Hansen from Show Low, and squatter Bill Scorse sold his stake to John L. Fish. By 1907, Lakeside had become a very saintly Mormon community, unlike its more secular neighbors three miles up the rutted road at Pinetop.

Abe and his family moved on the reservation along Corduroy Creek, a short distance from father-in-law Corydon E. Cooley.

McGuire said records show that Will Amos loaned a ton of salt to Fort Apache Indian agent C.W. Crouse. Will Amos also paid nominal fees to water his ewes on reservation land.

Crouse, however, wasn't too keen on Abe's and Will's two other brothers, Len and Dick. In 1906, according to McGuire, Crouse wrote them this letter:

"I would like to know by what authority you came on the Indian reservation and drove cattle away that you knew were not and are not yours. I have the proof that you drove not only (Chief) Alchesay's cow but others that were branded off the Indian reservation...I must tell you that your actions look bad in this matter...Under the circumstances I am obliged to forbid your coming to this reservation for any purpose whatever, and, I am sorry to make this order on account of your brother, W.N. (Will), whom I regard as a good man."

Fort Apache Indian agent C.W. Crouse, sitting in middle, with White Mountain Apache Council at Whiteriver. Circa: early 1900s.
Arizona Historical Society AHS# 11887

Living Among Apaches

In late August 1886, freight wagons rumbled past Phipps' saloon in Pinetop, bound for Holbrook. The cargo: nearly 400 Chiricahua Apache men, women and children being deported from Fort Apache to Florida. Their leader, Geronimo, and his hard-core band of warriors would follow from Fort Bowie less than two weeks later.

"I remember...how my father hauled a load of women and children off to Holbrook in his freight wagon, where they were then put on the train and sent to their prison home," recalls Rhoda P. Wakefield in James R. Jennings' book, *The Freight Rolled.*

"It must surely have seemed like a prison to them after being taken from the land of their fathers where they had roamed so freely."

The Apache Indians and residents of Pinetop have always been neighbors. The town's southern boundary borders the Fort Apache Indian Reservation, home of the White Mountain Apache Tribe. These Indians, for the most part, were peaceful during the Apache wars. Some, for no apparent reason, were deported to the San Carlos Indian Reservation but later allowed to return. White Mountain chiefs encouraged a fort to be built on their land for protection, and they wanted to live in peace with outsiders. For years, the Spaniards in the Southwest raided the Apaches and kidnapped their young and made them slaves. A fort, which was later named Fort Apache, was established in 1870, and cavalrymen rode across the mountains and through canyons trying to maintain peace.

The Apache tribes to the south and east of the White Mountain tribe were the main troublemakers, raiding and killing Indian and non-Indian alike. They also took non-Indians as slaves. Their leaders included Geronimo, Cochise and Victorio.

However, one band of White Mountain Indians did cause trouble that made national headlines. In 1881, an Apache medicine-man and prophet, Noch-ay-del-klinne, of the Cibecue band, professed the ability to raise the great Apache chiefs Diablo and Eskiole from the dead and, with their help, would drive the white men from Indian lands. These chiefs were killed in feuds between bands during the fall of 1880 and spring of 1881.

He also promised that the buffalo would return and the Indians would overcome all their ancient enemies. This charismatic prophet promised all this without bloodshed. This aroused intense excitement among the Apaches and the number of Noch-ay-del-klinne's followers grew.

Noch-ay-del-klinne, eight years earlier, had enlisted as an Indian scout at Camp (Fort) Apache for General George Crook's campaign against the hostile Apache Tontos. Later, Noch-ay-del-klinne accompanied a delegation of Apaches to Washington D.C., where each was given a peace medal by President Ulysses S. Grant.

Will C. Barnes, a soldier at Fort Apache during this time and author of *Apaches & Longhorns*, gives this account:

The brass in Washington D.C. got wind of Noch-ay-del-klinne's claims, including that he had a "ghost shirt" through which no white man's bullet could pass, and ordered the U.S. troops to arrest the medicine-man.

The Fort Apache general balked and said the Indian prophet was doing no harm and arresting him would only lead to trouble. He told his Washington boss that this "excitement will gradually exhaust itself."

The general was again ordered to go and make the arrest. Reluctantly, he left the fort with his officers and 67 enlisted men and six White Mountain Apache Indian scouts.

When the troops reached the Indian village on Cibecue Creek 45 miles west of Fort Apache, they arrested the medicine-man without incident. They moved four miles up the creek and made camp.

"Many Indians followed the troops," said Barnes, who was not part of the mission. "Several...Indian scouts had showed great anger over the arrest, and were even then talking together very earnestly. They were enlisted soldiers, and were, of course, fully armed."

Several Apaches entered the camp and the captain ordered them to leave. An Indian raised his rifle in a threatening way. "(The captain) turned to pick up his carbine. .(and) as he did so, one of the scouts shot him in the back, killing him instantly. The fight was on. Every scout joined his people in the attack."

The medicine-man tried to escape and was shot and killed. When darkness came and the fighting ended, four soldiers, including the officer, were dead and four more soldiers were seriously wounded. They later died. There are conflicting reports of how many Indians died. It could be as many as 17.

The killing didn't end with this battle at Cibecue. Barnes said that in one day, about a week later, the bodies of nine white men killed by the Apaches south of Fort Apache were found. They included four Mormons traveling to Utah; three soldiers operating a ferryboat on the Black River; a civilian scout from Fort Apache; and a man who herded steers for the beef-contractor at the fort.

The six Indian scouts who deserted at Cibecue were charged with desertion "to the enemy in battle." Five of them were captured. Three were hanged to death, and two went to Alcatraz military prison in San Francisco for a few years of confinement.

Unrest existed for a year between the White Mountain Apaches and the U.S. Army troops, but there were no more killings, Barnes said.

In September 1882, General George Crook was ordered to return to Arizona and take care of the situation between Indians and soldiers. Because of his fair dealings in the past, he was highly trusted by Indian and white men alike.

Apache leaders agreed to meet with him. Crook told them if they surrendered their weapons there would be no punishment. More than 100 Apaches came to the fort and laid their guns and cartridges in a huge pile.

"Peace has reigned between the White Mountain Apaches and the people of Arizona," Barnes wrote. "It was a triumph for Crook's tact and diplomacy. He knew his Apaches."

Crook's first big job was to conduct an exact count of all Indians, including children, on the reservation. With that task completed, he challenged the Indians to work for money. He offered the Indians one cent for every pound of grass they cut and $5 for every cord of wood they chopped and brought to the fort. In the first year, the Indians hauled more than 1,500 tons of hay they cut using small sickles or butcher-knives, and 600 cords of wood.

"Some of the Army contractors who had waxed fat on Army contracts at the posts raised a wail over Crook's scheme," Barnes wrote. "They pointed to the fact that much of the hay was simply green grass that had to be cured.

"Crook admitted this, but said the Indians were so busy getting (hay and wood) that they had neither time or inclination to fight or to raid the settlers, and that the soldiers were far better employed at scattering the grass out to dry in the stockyards than they would be in chasing a bunch of Apaches over Arizona mountains.

"General Crook taught these Indians to work; showed them the value of this labor, and proved to a rather skeptical world that, after all, the Apache Indians could and would work if given the chance and the proper guidance.

"...The post trader reaped a grand harvest in those days; for practically every dollar went into his store in exchange for calico, clothing, knives, mirrors and other articles dear to the Apache heart."

• • •

It is generally agreed that the Apaches and Navajos once were united. However, at some point, they went their separate ways. The Navajo cultivated the land for farming in the Four Corners area, but the Apaches continued their nomadic way of life south of them in the mountains and deserts of West Texas, New Mexico, Arizona and the upper part of Old Mexico.

The Apaches sometimes fought each other and other Indian tribes. These bands included the White Mountain (Coyoteros), Pinals, Warm Springs, Tontos, Mimbres, Chiricahuas, Rio Verdes and Aravaipas Apaches.

As white men moved into Indian lands, the Apaches became hemmed in. Mexicans fought them on the south and white settlers on the north. In 1870, the Apaches were placed on a reservation called San Carlos, an empire of over 100 square miles. A year later, President Ulysses S. Grant signed an executive order that carved the northern half of the San Carlos preserve into the Fort Apache Indian Reservation, a 1,664,874-acre bountiful forest land bordered on the north by the Mogollon Rim and on the south by the Salt and Black rivers.

Fort Apache military post was built to oversee the White Mountain Indians. Martha Summerhayes, wife of an U.S. cavalry officer, lived at the fort from October 1874 to April 1875. Her glimpses of the White Mountain Apaches are recorded in her book, *Vanished Arizona*.

She called these Indians "a fierce and cruel tribe, whose depredations and atrocities had been carried on for years, in and around, and, indeed far away from their mountain homes.

"But this tribe was now under surveillance of the (U.S.) Government, and guarded by a strong garrison of cavalry and infantry at Camp (later named Fort) Apache. They were divided into bands, under Chiefs Pedro, Diablo, Patone and Cibiano."

She said these Indians came into the post twice a week to be counted and to receive their rations of beef, sugar, beans and other staples.

"Large stakes were driven into the ground; at each stake, sat or stood the leader of a band; a sort of father to his people; then the rest of them stretched out in several long lines, young bucks and old ones, squaws and pappooses, the families together, about 1,700 souls in all.

"...The squaws looked at our clothes and chuckled, and made some of their inarticulate remarks to each other. The bucks looked admiringly at the white women, especially at the cavalry beauty, Mrs. Montgomery, although I thought that Chief Diablo cast a special eye at our young Mrs. Bailey, of the infantry.

"Diablo was a handsome fellow. I was especially impressed by his extraordinary good looks.

"...The young lieutenants sometimes tried to make up to the prettiest (Indian girls), and offered them trinkets, pretty boxes of soap, beads and small mirrors (so dear to the heart of the Indian girl), but the young maids were coy enough; it seemed to me they cared more for men of their own race."

Summerhayes said a soldier brought in the mail, which was from two to three weeks old, on horseback twice a week. One mail-carrier was killed by Indians and the mail destroyed.

Chief Diablo
Arizona Historical Society AHS# 926

One evening the officers and wives were invited to an Indian dance at a nearby ravine. Fires blazed while "hordes of wild Apaches darted about, while others sat on logs beating...tomtoms," Summerhayes wrote

The dancers wore loincloths; their bodies were painted and feathers were tied from their elbows and knees. Upon their heads were large frames, made to resemble elk horns. The dancing stopped and the arena was cleared.

"Two wicked-looking creatures came out and performed a sort of shadow dance, brandishing knives as they glided through the intricate figures.

"...Suddenly the shouts became warhoops, the demons brandished their knives madly, and nodded their branching horns; the tomtoms were beaten with a dreadful din, and terror seized my heart. What if they be treacherous, and had lured our small party down into this ravine for an ambush!"

The white women were frightened and left.

Another time, Major Worth, a bachelor, threw a party in his quarters and invited the officers and their wives and the chiefs and their "harems."

"A quadrille was formed, in which the chiefs danced opposite the officers. The squaws sat around as they were too shy to dance. These chiefs were painted, and wore only their necklaces and the customary loincloth, throwing their blankets about their shoulders when they had finished dancing. I noticed again Chief Diablo's great good looks.

"...Diablo was charmed with the young, handsome wife of one of the officers, and asked her husband how many ponies he would take for her, and Pedro asked Major Worth, if all those white squaws belonged to him."

• Jennings, in *The Freight Rolled* book, reports that freighters in the late 1800s and early 1900s often told stories of the extreme hunger that existed among some of the Indians.

Chief Pedro
Arizona Historical Society   AHS# 62540

"On one occasion a group or family of Indians sat in a ranch yard where the ranchers were killing beef. After the task was completed and the beef removed, the Indians—men, women and children—pounced upon the entrails, eating them raw with gusto."

He added:

"The Indian children were afraid of us. The Indians seemed to be constantly on the move, riding horses in groups of three to five. The male member of the family rode a horse while the squaw and children walked behind. The squaw carried the camp belongings which were packed in a canvas larger than a bed sheet and looped over the forehead, the pack hanging on the back. She also carried the nursing baby. Babies were strapped into a cradleboard and carried on the back of the mother."

These observations by Barnes, Summerhayes and Jennings occurred more than 100 years ago. Traveling on the Fort Apache Indian Reservation today is a far cry from the life of Indians in the late 1800s. Site-built homes abound instead of tepees and wickiups, and schools and healthcare facilities have been constructed.

The White Mountain Apaches harvest timber and produce lumber at sawmills, and they have built a heavy tourist trade that includes fishing in man-made lakes; hunting wild game throughout the mountains, meadows and canyons; skiing at Sunrise Ski Resort, and; yes, gambling at the ever-expanding casino at Hon-Dah, just three miles from the heart of Pinetop.

Apache youths at Pinetop's Fall Festival

Jake Renfro

Winters can be extremely severe in the White Mountains, as Jake Renfro and his family experienced some 75 years ago.

Jake, his wife and two children, along with a neighbor child, became stranded in their car in one of the worst blizzards ever to hit the White Mountains.

"Jake got out of the car and started to walk the many miles to town on the deserted road," writes Sharon George, Jake's granddaughter, in her family-history journal. "Blanche (Jake's wife) stayed in the car and kept the children awake for more than two days. She knew that if they were to fall asleep in their freezing condition, they would all die.

"She pinched, slapped and even resorted to setting their hair on fire then quickly slapping it out, of course, to keep them awake.

"In the meantime, Jake had stumbled into town and collapsed after telling their location."

A rescue party quickly formed and found the snow-covered car and brought the occupants to safety—and warmth.

Ralph Thurston "Jake" Renfro was born Feb. 4, 1897 in Oklahoma. He served in World War I in France, where he suffered from mustard-gas poisoning. He came home to a veterans' hospital in Denver, where his family thought he would die.

Instead of dying, he recovered with the help of Blanche Palmburg, a nurses' aide, who nursed him back to health. They fell in love and were married April 10, 1919 They had two children, which they named after themselves: Ralph Thurston born in 1920 and Blanche Ione born in 1922. The family moved to Pinetop when their two children "weren't very old," probably in the mid or late 1920s.

"I remember my mother saying that they were the first "gentiles," or non-Mormons, to move into the small community," said Sharon George.

Renfro pulled two log cabins together and opened a cafe.

"Jake loved to fish, and spent a lot of time with the many friends that he made," she said. "But, friends weren't all that he made. He also made moonshine whiskey and sold it to the local people and throughout the whole four-corner area during Prohibition. This is one thing that he had in common with his Renfro cousins in Oklahoma and Kansas; they all seemed to be involved in making and selling moonshine whiskey and they all loved to fish!

"Jake had many friends who warned him when the law or the 'revenuers' were coming. In the wintertime, Jake stashed his jars or baking-powder tins of money, mostly coins, outside the windows in the deep snow banks. He was never caught for doing this.

"When Prohibition was repealed (in 1933), Jake opened a legitimate business and called it 'Jake Renfro's Famous Log Cabin Cafe'."

Blanche, who was known as an excellent cook, often ran the cafe alone, which she resented, when Jake spent a

Jake and Blanche Renfro

lot of time fishing and hunting or guiding fishing and hunting parties.

One time, when an airplane crashed on the top of Mount Baldy about 25 miles southeast of Pinetop, Jake and Blanche went with the rescue crew to cook for the men at a base camp. The rescuers had to retrieve the bodies and belongings of the victims and bring them down from the mountain, which took a long time to accomplish.

In 1938, Jake sold the cafe to Charlie Clark and moved his family to Phoenix. Later, the couple opened a restaurant in Boise, Idaho. They moved back to Pinetop for a short time, where relatives lived, but moved away again. On June 29, 1951, Jake died in Ajo, Arizona. He, along with his daughter, mother, granddaughter and half-sister are buried in the Pinetop cemetery.

"I was his oldest living grandchild at the time of his death," recalls Sharon George. "...He liked The Sons of the Pioneers, and he sang *The Big Rock Candy Mountain* to me. He loved his dog, Ginger, and gave him a wristwatch to wear. He fixed me a small sled, and let Ginger pull me on it."

Charlie Clark's

Charlie Clark's Steak House is undeniably the most famous landmark in Pinetop. It's been there since 1938.

Actually, the establishment had its start long before Charlie Clark ever showed up in town. Sometime during Prohibition (1920-33), Jake Renfro moved two log cabins

Charlie Clark opened his steakhouse and bar in 1938

together, one of which was an old Penrod house, and opened up "Jake Renfro's Famous Log Cabin Cafe," said Frank Crosby, Charlie Clark's son-in-law.

"Charlie and other people told me about the start of Charlie Clark's," he said. "Pinetop was a little, bitty town, six or eight families, during Prohibition."

During this time Renfro bootlegged whiskey out of his "cafe," Crosby said.

Crosby recalls mopping the floor in Charlie Clark's more than 50 years ago, while an old-timer named Stewart sat at the bar watching him.

The old-timer pointed to a spot on the barroom floor.

"'Jake had a wooden barrel to keep whiskey in there,'" Crosby quoted the old-timer. "'When we came in to get a drink he would pump it to get whiskey out of there (even) when we wanted a bottle to take home.'"

Renfro built additions to the two original cabins, enlarging the restaurant and bar. The two cabins are hidden inside the structure even to this day, Crosby said.

Renfro brought in penny, nickel, dime and quarter slot machines for the gambling and drinking crowd.

While Renfro was operating his rockin' club in "downtown" Pinetop, Charlie Clark ranched in the lonely stretches of grassland some 40 miles north of Pinetop at Mesa Redondo, near Concho.

Charlie Clark was born Aug. 15, 1886 in Ohio. His mother died when he was 12, and two years later his father remarried. Charlie disliked his stepmother and ran away from home. He moved to Michigan, leaving behind a brother and two sisters whom he never saw or spoke to again the rest of his life.

"He wouldn't tell you his folks' name and things about his birth," Crosby said. "He wouldn't say much about his childhood."

While in Detroit he worked for Henry Ford. Charlie told people he would have become a millionaire had he stuck with Ford.

Charlie Clark

"He did tell me about his coming to Arizona," Crosby said. "As a teenager, he cowboyed near Willcox. The grass was up to the horses' bellies."

Later, he homesteaded land near Concho.

"I don't know where he met his wife (Belle Wilson) but she came from Ireland," Crosby said.

The couple had two daughters, Dolly and Marguerite Elizabeth, the latter known as "Buddy." In 1934, at age 37, Belle died, leaving Charlie to raise the two girls alone.

"She had thrombosis," recalled Buddy nearly 70 years later. "I guess a blood vessel broke because she turned purple in the face.

"She had washed (clothes) that morning; she didn't feel well and my father needed to go to a campsite. They were branding cattle. My sister was the one who found her and she came to the back door and screamed."

Charlie Clark ranched for four years after his wife died before moving to town. During this time he rented a house in Holbrook where his daughters lived while attending high school. Charlie visited his daughters on weekends.

Buddy recalls how hard her father's life was after her mother died.

"He was so lonely...he just couldn't take it any more."

Charlie sold his ranch. For a while he didn't know what to do with his life or money.

Buddy said he thought about buying the cabins and a restaurant at Indian Pine (now Hon-Dah) but decided instead to buy Jake Renfro's nightclub and renaming it after himself.

This was May of 1938, the same month Buddy graduated from Holbrook High School.

When Charlie bought out Jake Renfro's, he also inherited the slot machines. Buddy emptied the slots and counted the money. She watched some of the lumberjacks in the area losing their entire $10 paychecks at one time on the slots.

During this time, another nightclub stood next door to Charlie Clark's.

While Charlie and Buddy were in Tempe a week after Charlie bought his place, picking up Dolly from Arizona State College, the bar burned down.

Buddy Wise

People formed a bucket brigade from an irrigation ditch about 50 yards away, but the attempt to put out the blaze was useless.

"I used to go over there and find nickels because they had slot machines, too," Buddy said.

The bar, where The Burly Bear now stands, was never rebuilt. However, the Ponderosa Club was later built just west of The Burly Bear. It too burned down in the 1980s and today is still an empty lot. (Ironically, the huge tree that was in front of the Ponderosa Club, which still stands today, is not a Ponderosa pine, but a fir tree.)

During the 1940s, dances were held Saturday nights at Charlie Clark's. A druggist from McNary by the name of Beagle came in to play the piano. When he wasn't there, musicians who played the saxophone and trombone would entertain.

She recalls riding with her father to Fort Apache to pick up 50-pound blocks of ice to keep the beer cool in Charlie Clark's. This was before refrigerators came on the scene.

Buddy describes her father as a "very fair man." He was a hard worker, being the cook at his establishment and running "the whole show." In 1942, Charlie married Thelma Wetzel Runge, daughter of Mabel Bowles, who owned much of the land at that time in Pinetop.

Buddy followed her sister and attended classes at Arizona State College. The girls came home to Pinetop on summer vacations and on holidays. After graduation, Buddy moved away, taught for a year, joined the Army, married Tom Wise, raised a son (named Charlie after his grandfather) and lived mostly in the Eastern United States. She moved back to Pinetop after her father died.

But her sister chose another path. After Dolly graduated from college she moved to McNary to teach in the local high school. She also spent time at her father's restaurant. It was during this time she met Frank Crosby.

Crosby was born in 1917 in New Mexico and, when he was only six months old, his father was struck by lightning and killed. His mother and her six children moved to St. Johns, Arizona.

As a young man Crosby moved to McNary to work. He lived in a boarding house with other single men.

"That was before World War II," Crosby said. "The favorite place for everyone was Charlie Clark's. There wasn't any place in McNary. You couldn't buy a drink or anything on the (Fort Apache) reservation.

"Everyone in McNary came down to Pinetop to do their partying."

And Dolly became part of his life. They began dating.

The United States entered World War II and Crosby enlisted in the Army, but he didn't know how long it would be before the military would call him for active duty. Frank and Dolly couldn't decide whether to get married before he went into the service or wait until the war was over.

One night Frank, Dolly and another young couple sat together at a table in Charlie Clark's. They closed the place at 1 a.m. The young couple told Frank and Dolly that if they were really serious about getting married, they should do it that night. The couple knew a Mormon bishop in Holbrook who also was the clerk of the court.

"We went to Holbrook (and) went to his house and woke him up," Crosby said. "Bless his heart, he went down to the courthouse, wrote us out a marriage license and married us. This was 3 or 4 o'clock in the morning."

They spent the day in St. Johns and then the next day drove back to McNary.

"I insisted that we stop and tell Charlie," Crosby said. "My wife was reluctant; she didn't want to tell (her father). We stopped and I went in and Charlie was sweeping the floor. I said, 'Charlie, Dolly and I got married.' And he said, 'Humph, that's what you want to do,' and he turned away and walked off. That was the last time he spoke to me for months."

About a year later, Crosby was called to active duty. He and Charlie by this time were friends and were on speaking terms. While Crosby was stationed in Seattle,

Charlie got sick and had to go to the Mayo Clinic in Minnesota. He needed someone to run his establishment.

Crosby said Charlie was a close friend of Arizona Senator Carl Hayden. Charlie persuaded the senator to pull some army strings so Crosby could take three weeks' leave to return to Pinetop and run Charlie Clark's.

"There wasn't much business then. It was a slow time of the year."

When the war was over and Crosby moved back to the White Mountains, Charlie offered his son-in-law a job at Charlie Clark's.

"I worked for him for quite a while, maybe a year (or) two, and he said, 'Son, do you like a partnership in this business?' And I said 'I'd love it,' and we made an agreement."

Crosby said he didn't take home much money, because what he did earn went back to Charlie as his share of buying into the business.

Crosby smiles about the stories Charlie told him about the slots he had in his bar. Actually, during this time, slots were all over Arizona, and Globe-Miami was full of them, Crosby said. They were illegal, but if you paid off a law officer you could operate them for a profit.

"So, when the sheriff came around for pay-off, Charlie said, 'No, screw you.' He had to take the slots out," Crosby said.

First, he turned the 10 to 12 slots to face the wall and later put them in storage. After a few years, Crosby said he thinks Charlie had him haul the slots to a service organization in Springerville.

Crosby recalls that before the concrete floors were poured in Charlie Clark's, the skunks loved to crawl under the wooden floor "and stink up the place."

He said Charlie had a jukebox hooked up to a power plant on the premises.

"Anytime anybody played it, it started the power plant and he (Charlie) said, 'I'm not going to start the power plant for a nickel.'"

Charlie plugged up the nickel slot and people had to use a dime or quarter to play the jukebox.

"People would play that jukebox and dance and have a lot of fun."

Charlie bought whole loins of beef and hung them inside the kitchen area to age. When someone ordered a steak, Charlie would hoist up a hindquarter and carry it to the kitchen table. People sitting at the bar could see Charlie through the open kitchen door cutting the steaks. He sold the steaks by the pound.

"He did all this after you ordered so we could sell you a few drinks," said Crosby, adding sometimes Charlie would wait until the customer had had at least two drinks before he would put the steak on the grill.

"The money was in the bar," Crosby said.

Charlie hung a huge sign on his building that announced: "Charlie Clark's Log Cabin Cafe."

"When the wind would blow it would swing, swing, swing," Crosby said.

"(Charlie) pretty much was all business," Crosby said. "He wasn't happy-go-lucky at all. Charlie never got the cowboy out of him. He always had a horse and he always had cattle. When he died we sold off the remaining cattle."

Charlie ran his cattle in a pasture across the street from his steakhouse.

Charlie Clark died of prostate cancer April 12, 1953, at age 66. He and his second wife, Thelma Wetsel Clark (Dec. 12, 1894-Aug. 2, 1952), are buried in a private cemetery for Pinetop pioneers at the end of Penrod Lane, just down the road from Charlie Clark's Steak House.

Even in death mystery surrounds the life of Charlie Clark. His tombstone lists his birth as 1887, but his death certificate states he was born in 1886.

To this day Charlie's saddle is on display in Crosby's living room in Pinetop.

After Charlie's death, Crosby ran Charlie Clark's for a few years.

During this time, Walsh Mack, who had worked in McNary, opened the Dew Drop Inn down the main highway from Charlie Clark's.

"Once in a while I'd sneak in there to get some barbecue beef," said Crosby, adding that he avoided the place when it was crowded because it could get "rough."

"There were several big fights in there and there have been one or two people killed," he said.

Crosby sold Charlie Clark's twice. The first owner failed to make payments, so Crosby had to take it back. The second owner sold it to a "softball queen...I can't remember her name," he said.

It is unknown how many times Charlie Clark's changed owners. In 1975, a Chinese couple bought it and renamed the establishment Dragon Inn. The next owner changed the name back to Charlie Clark's.

Dub and Virginia Bickel sold the restaurant to its present owner, Bill Gibson, in 1981. Virginia Bickel was Gibson's sixth grade teacher.

Gibson and his parents ran cattle and operated a mini-storage business in the Phoenix area. The family vacationed in the White Mountains and built a mini-storage unit here. Gibson learned Charlie Clark's was for sale and he bought it.

Gibson renovated and enlarged the place through the years. He developed a 2 1/2 acre apple orchard just south of Charlie Clark's, where Oktoberfest and other events are held.

Gibson recalls that through the years the place has had its share of fires and floods.

During one flood the water rose eight to 10 inches and customers climbed onto the tables.

Gibson said one day he came off the golf course and while driving by he saw smoke coming from Charlie Clark's attic. He went up there to put out the fire but passed out. A fireman carried him out.

More recently, in the summer of 2003, a fire started in the outside trash bin and spread to the building, destroying part of the structure. Gibson said he believes the fire was caused by an arsonist. A waitress said she was told cigarette butts from the restaurant were dumped into the trash bin and that might have started the fire. After several months the damage was repaired and the restaurant was expanded to include Gibson's Room, a private dining room for up to 12 people, and new office space.

Gibson recalls another time when the ceiling began to collapse in the bar.

"The old timers put their hands over their drinks and the new customers put their hands over their heads," Gibson said.

Gibson and other oldtimers at the restaurant tell stories of strange happenings at Charlie Clark's. Could there be ghosts? they wonder.

One night, a bartender closed up the empty building and a man appeared at the pool table. Another time music came out of a closed room that was padlocked.

One time a picture "jumped off the wall" eight feet and hit a man in the back of the head, Gibson said.

Ghosts or not, Charlie Clark's popularity grows each year. Recently, 35 tons of prime rib were served in just one year.

"We are known pretty much around the world," Gibson said. He hears reports of people talking about Charlie Clark's in Europe and Asia.

Some of the celebrities who have dined at Charlie Clark's have been John Wayne, David Spade, Willie Nelson, George Strait, Hermit Hermits, golfer Jack Nicklaus and Kareem Abdul-Jabbar, the basketball superstar who spent time in the White Mountains as an assistant high school basketball coach on the nearby Indian reservation.

"He was so tall his head nearly hit the ceiling," recalls one restaurant worker.

Bill Gibson admits the smartest thing he ever did while owning Charlie Clark's was to marry one of his waitresses.

"(Tricia) married the boss; she's the one who is the glue and holds the whole thing together," one worker observed.

In the waiting area in Charlie Clark's is a large bronze relief of Bill Gibson, which was presented to him by his wife on April 8, 2001 to congratulate him on owning/operating Charlie Clark's for 20 years.

The last part of the inscription jokingly notes: "We all know that without his wife, Tricia Gibson, running the whole place behind the scenes, Bill would have probably gone broke years ago."

Bill and Tricia Gibson

Walsh Mack

Pinetop old-timers have fond memories of Walsh Mack, a Black man whose Dew Drop Inn in Pinetop during the 1940s and 50s arguably served up the best barbecue ribs west of New Orleans. John Wayne, who with a partner owned a ranch down the road toward Springerville, liked to drop in and chat with his friend Mack.

Frank Crosby, who in the '50s owned Charlie Clark's Steak House down the road, confessed that once in a while he would sneak away and show up inside Dew Drop Inn to eat some ribs.

Dew Drop Inn was more than just a rib-selling place—it boasted of being a swinging saloon and dance hall, too. Sometimes the place became rowdy and fights broke out, and reports came out about a killing or two throughout the years.

Jo Baeza, a newspaper reporter with the *White Mountain Independent*, has written many historical stories on the area, including those about Walsh Mack and the famous Dew Drop Inn. Most of the following information was gleaned from her articles that appeared through the years in the *Independent*.

The first time Baeza met Mack was while a teenager living in Holbrook. She wrote:

"A car full of us decided to drive down to Pinetop and hit the Dew Drop Inn. Nobody told us most people considered it 'off limits' to white kids in 1950. When we walked through the door everybody stopped talking. Not a good sign. We kids were standing there looking real white and real stupid when a giant of a man walked toward us. He was 6-foot-4 with shoulders like Joe Louis and hands the size of bear paws. He put one paw around my shoulders and led us in. He said, 'Now, there ain't gonna be any trouble, but if there is, you all get behind me.'"

Walsh Mack was born in Louisiana in 1891. He only got a fourth-grade education and then went out to help his parents support the family. He left home at 18 and first worked in a livery stable and afterward in a sawmill and steel foundry. He served in the U.S. Army during World War I.

On Jan. 17, 1924, Mack stepped off the train in Holbrook and "wished to hell" as he stood shivering on the station platform that he'd never left home. He didn't have enough money to turn around and head back to a warmer Louisiana. Instead, he climbed aboard another train bound for McNary to work in the lumber mill. At times the train crept along and Mack got off and walked along the tracks to pass the time.

At McNary, he worked as a lumber grader, millwright, oiler and log scaler. Mack and other African Americans lived in the segregated community of Milltown, away from the Anglos, Hispanics and Indians. They all had their separate communities.

In Milltown, Dollie Sells owned a small cafe. She and Mack married in 1934. The couple bought property in Pinetop from Mabel Bowles, "who didn't give a hoot what color they were."

Walsh and Dollie Mack

There were influential people in the area who were enraged over the sale. Mack was fired from his job at the mill and Dollie lost her lease on her Milltown cafe. The Macks moved to Pinetop and built a small cafe.

But hatred still abounded. One Easter Sunday unknown persons set fire to their cafe and burned it down.

"Walsh was a good member of the community," said Ermina Henning of Pinetop. "He was well-liked." She remembered her minister saying in church one Sunday after Mack's place was set ablaze: "It's hard for me to call some of you people Christians after the way you've treated Walsh Mack."

The Macks refused to be run out of town and with $125.50 they had saved, they bought some reject lumber and began rebuilding. At their new cafe they sold hamburgers, chile, barbecued ribs, chicken gumbo, pies and bread. The first few weeks they grossed 10 to 25 cents a day. Nine years later the couple's ventures included a grocery store, cafe and liquor store that brought in $200,000 in a year.

Eventually, Mack sold the Dew Drop Inn to John Crosser and after that the place changed hands many times. It burned down in 1975 and was rebuilt, apparently using some unburned lumber.

Mack got restless not owning a business, so he started other eateries. He moved into a building now called The Lion's Den and called his new place Pinetop Buffet and Bar-B-Q. The large building contained a cafe, bar, dance floor and pool hall. It thrived during the 1960s and early 70s.

"He treated everyone with respect but took no guff," wrote Baeza in the *Independent* on Feb. 20, 2004. "He was the first to help someone sick, old, out of work, or stranded. He listened with a patient yawn while his bar patrons told him their wives didn't understand them. He went to church, fulfilled his Masonic obligations, and cooked for the Sheriff's Posse."

After his wife died, Mack lost interest in business. He cooked and took the food to others, especially those who lived alone. Pinetop residents Joe and Sarah Mason remember Mack in the 1970s spending time in the country store across from Charlie Clark's talking about the history of the area to anyone who would stop by to listen. And sometimes there were knots of people hanging onto his every word.

In 1979, Mack moved to California. He died a few years later in Los Angeles at age 92.

In 1982, however, workers tore down the re-built Dew Drop Inn and hauled the lumber away for other uses. In the eyes of Pinetop's old timers, a part of what reminded them of Mack went with it.

Mike Wilton said when he bought his Lakeside house in the 1990s he was told that a wooden floor beam under his house had bullet holes in it. "I was told I could see them if I wanted to crawl under the house," Wilton said. That beam came from Dew Drop Inn.

Lakeside

Between the time Corydon E. Cooley and Marion Clark settled in Show Low in the early 1870s and the arrival of Johnny Phipps in Pinetop in 1885, there were perhaps a half-dozen other small log cabins widely scattered in the forest from Show Low to McNary.

Those living here were of Indian, Anglo or Anglo-Indian origin. One was a red-haired Irishman named Kelley, who had six sons living on Porter Creek. There was a man named Springer, probably a trapper, who lived on Billy Creek. After giving his name to Springer Mountain, he left the area. About 1878, George, James and Robert Scott, Bill Morgan and Jim Porter herded sheep into the area.

Another family reportedly lived in a two-room cabin at the base of Pinetop Mountain just south of Rim Road. Anna Jackson, interviewed in *Lakeside Locale,* a Blue Ridge Junior High School project in 1985, said the cabin had a blanket for a door and flour sacks for windows.

One night, while the mother and her two babies and teenaged son were in bed, an Indian man crept in. The mother and son remained quiet, feigning sleep.

"As soon as the mother saw him she knew it was the feared Apache Kid. Jim (the boy) also saw him." The

The Apache Kid
Arizona Historical Society AHS# 17776

Apache Kid glanced at the babies and then the mother. He went into the second room, looked around and then walked out. He looked at Jim and the rifle aside the bed. He then left the cabin.

The mother and Jim were very shaken, but they hopped out of bed and peeked out the window. They saw the Apache Kid, his horse, and about nine other Indians. They apparently were looking for kidnapped Indian maidens. The Indians left, and after this the mother refused to return to the cabin.

During the 1880s, more settlers arrived and staked homestead claims on the Mountain. About three miles southwest of Pinetop, around 1890, a few ranches began springing up. The settlers first called this area Fairview, then Hog Town (because couple farmers let their pigs run amuck in the forest), and, finally, Woodland.

Hans Hansen, the Mormon bishop of the Show Low Ward, moved to the Warren Ranch between Pinetop and Woodland in 1891. It was on the Warren Ranch that Eph Penrod met Mary Jane Hansen, and they were married December 1892 at Woodland. The following year, Hans Hansen moved to Woodland and he and his son, Hans Hansen Jr., practiced their chosen trade as mason and brick layer. The father-son team did the rock work at Fort Apache, Whiteriver and for nearly all the two-story brick houses in the area.

It was during this time and into the 1900s that Loretta Hansen, wife of Hans Hansen Jr., became a sought-after midwife, traveling throughout the area including Pinetop to help bring newborns into the world. There were no doctors from Holbrook to Whiteriver at the time, and it was not uncommon that she was called upon by the homesteaders for medical assistance. She was in frail health much of the time, and sometimes she was sicker than the person she went to assist with her nursing skills.

Others who lived in Woodland in the 1890s included Al Young, Al Young Jr., Joseph Stock, Aleck McCleve and Abner Crandall. (It was Al Young and McCleve who raised the hogs at the time the settlement was called Hog Town. This was short-lived: Mormon Stake President Jessie N. Smith didn't think that name sounded appropriate and he changed the name to Woodland.)

Hans Hansen

The Mormons officially began meeting in November of 1893, with Hans Hansen Jr. as superintendent of Sunday School. (A formal church in the area was formed in 1912, when the Lakeside Ward of the Church of Jesus Christ of Latter-day Saints was organized.)

Another person who lived in the area in the 1890s was Billy Scorse, an Englishman, for whom Billy Creek was

Billy Scorse

named. He owned 40 acres in what is now the heart of downtown Lakeside, and he had squatter's rights to more land in the area. He built a saloon, advertising it as the "Last Chance" for anyone to get liquor if they're heading for Holbrook or beyond. (Pinetop had a saloon farther east that was owned by Johnny Phipps and later Walt Rigney and Albert Penrod) The 60-mile journey between Scorse's enterprise and Holbrook traversed through the liquor-dry Mormon territory that included Show Low, Taylor and Snowflake.

In 1903, Show Low's W.J. Flake traded Adair Spring to William Amos, a sheepherder, for 102 acres on Show Low Creek to be used as a storage reservoir. (A dam was constructed five years earlier, but heavy rains washed it away.) In the fall of 1903, men with picks and shovels began work on the new dam, which was completed in December 1904. Later, another five feet was added to the dam's height.

The major reason for the creation of Rainbow Lake, and later for Scott's Reservoir a few miles northeast, was for storage of irrigation water for Show Low farmers. A severe drought had taken hold of the White Mountains and all the springs dried up except Adair Spring.

In 1905, the sheep market bottomed out and the sheepmen decided to sell their properties.

Niels Hansen, one of the six Mormon colonizers in Show Low, wanted to buy some of this land. He went to Mormon Bishop James Clark Owens of Show Low and asked him if he should buy the land himself or buy the land with other people. Owens advised him to buy it alone, and Owens and Robert Scott provided the security for Hansen's loan. He bought out the holdings of Will Amos. John L. Fish bought out Billy Scorse (who then moved to Pinetop and later to California). Joseph Peterson and Alof Pratt Larson bought land on the southwest part of the lake that belonged to Mr. and Mrs. Amos, who homesteaded the area along with their four sons. The senior Amos had died and his widow wanted to leave the area. Other Mormon colonists moved in, buying out other properties. Thus, a Mormon community formed.

Fish opened a small store where Scorse's saloon had been.

One Spring day in 1906, six men—Hansen, Fish, John Heber Hansen, Peterson, Louis E. Johnson and Larson—sat in the sun and decided to name this new community "Lakeside." Peterson's daughter, Leora Peterson Schuck, said in her autobiography that her father suggested the name.

On Oct. 5, 1906, Lakeside became "official." A Lakeside Post Office opened with Fish as postmaster. (Pinetop's post office opened in 1891, and Show Low's in 1880.)

Niels Hansen

Lakeside residents named Niels Hansen the community's first mayor. He was noted for his surveying ability. Many times people told him that water would not run where he surveyed, but he would only reply, "Never you mind. Plough your ditch where the stakes are and your water will run." And he was right.

Hansen's house had a cistern, or open well, fed by an ditch from Adair Spring. As more people moved into the community, Hansen and his family had to get up early each morning to let the water flow into the well. If they opened the ditch's floodgate too late, the water would be somewhat dirty. Upstream people would wade in it, cows and horses would drink from it and dogs would play in it.

Niels Hansen's house came around full circle. When he lived in Show Low, where he was one of the Mormon colonizers of that town, he built Will Amos house out of adobe for $300. When Amos put up the "For Sale" sign, Hansen bought the house he built.

"Uncle Niels was a jolly man who was fond of children and had an unusually optimistic nature," said Schuck. "He stood a trifle one-sided like the leaning Tower of Pisa because a childhood accident had caused one leg to grow slightly shorter than the other."

He built several rowboats, including the oars, which allowed the first families of Lakeside to enjoy cruising on Rainbow Lake.

The people of Lakeside became a close-knit group. They celebrated their first Christmas party in Niels Hansen's living room. A small gift hung on the tree for each person who lived in Lakeside. Carols were sung and the town's populace "feasted on their simple foods."

Lakeside residents, as late as 1925, still celebrated Christmas in Niels and Belle Hansen's house Lorenzo Lisonbee, who spent part of his youth in Lakeside, noted in his memoirs that Santa Claus arrived on Christmas Eve at the house and handed out gifts to all the children. Hansen died in 1933 at the age of 64. His wife died in 1942 at the age of 67.

Sawmills flourished in the tri-town area (Pinetop-Woodland-Lakeside). Several mills were built along Billy Creek. A Mr. Fowler built one near Pinetop, but Niels Hansen and others bought it and moved it to Lakeside.

There used to be a sawmill where the Christmas Tree restaurant is now located.

By 1910, a total of 114 people lived in Lakeside, with that number swelling to 225 in 1920. By now, Woodland, along with the sawmill community of Milltown across Billy Creek north of where Blue Ridge High School is now located, became part of Lakeside.

Leora Peterson Schuck left Lakeside in the 1920s, moving back in 1960. She observed:

"Lakeside had changed to an unbelievable degree from what it had been in my childhood. No longer was it one big family. The woods were full of houses, and strangers...Sunday meetings were full of summer visitors and contained more strangers than acquaintances."

She left the Mountain again, returning in 1976:

"This population has increased year by year until now in 1976 people swarm up and down...and on all the lakes from Show Low to Maverick. Campers and motor homes abound; roads are as crowded with traffic as city streets.

Rhoton Barn in Lakeside today

Leora Peterson Schuck

Real estate salesmen have proliferated to unheard of numbers, businesses have flocked in, hundreds of people have come permanent residents, and the Chamber of Commerce scarcely closes its collective eye in the campaign for more. Oh, me, I wish it would stop."

Schuck continued: "Friends do not drop in as they do when one is young, yet one needs them more. In my long absence from Lakeside people forgot me, and just say hello and goodby at church. My loyal neighbor Anna is the exception. She comes occasionally with her husband Gilmore (Jackson) and they spend an evening. I wish they would come oftener...at church I dangle on the fringes. Our ward has many new people, young couples with children who keep them busy. This summer I have not had a home teacher at all, only a few heretofore."

Schuck lived out her days in Lakeside, dying in 1986 at the age of 85. She is buried in the Lakeside Cemetery.

McNary

McNary is seven miles southeast of Pinetop on the Fort Apache Indian Reservation. At one time, it was the largest town in the White Mountains.

The townsite originally was called Cluff Cienega and a post office with that name was established.

Tom Pollock, a rich Flagstaff entrepreneur and a partner, invested heavily in building a sawmill there in 1917. He was spurred by the high lumber prices during World War I. The vast forests in the White Mountains and Indian reservation provided plenty of lumber. In fact, at that time, several private sawmills operated near Pinetop and Lakeside and the area was known as "Sawmill Valley."

Pollock and the partner built a railroad—"The Apache Railway"—from Holbrook to the sawmill. He also built much of the town. In 1919, he changed the town's name to Cooley, after Corydon E. Cooley, an Indian scout who later became the official notary for Pinetop and surrounding areas.

Then the bottom fell out. The country entered a recession and lumber prices fell. His Apache Lumber Company closed down and his creditors took over.

In 1923, after having cleared their interests in Louisiana's forests, M.W. Cady and James G. McNary looked elsewhere. They purchased the interests of Pollock's lumber mill in Cooley. They continued to lease the town from the Apache Tribe and they brought in their experienced employees, mostly African Americans, to supplement local Anglo, Hispanic and Indian workers.

The new owners changed the name of the town to McNary in 1924. The expanded lumber operations became known as Southwest Forest Industries. The mill in its heyday employed more than 700 workers. The town grew to about 3,000 people. Teenagers from Pinetop even went to high school there.

The houses and buildings in this company town on Indian land were painted a uniform brown. The town's amenities included a general store, commissary, shops, movie theater, pool hall, bowling alley, gas station, bank, garage, a hospital, clinic and post office. People from throughout the White Mountains came there to be entertained, shop and to have babies and get healed at the only hospital in the area. The McNary theater was moved to Pinetop and now serves as an antique shop.

Dr. Arnold Dysterheft, a country doctor, practiced at the clinic and hospital for many years. The outpatient case load soared to more than 40,000 visits a year and the practice outgrew the facilities. Dr. Dysterheft, who died in 1999 at the age of 87, led the way for the establishment of Navapache Regional Medical Center in Show Low. The hospital and clinic in McNary closed in the 1970s.

McNary segregated its townsfolk. Anglo families lived in homes on the hill north of town. African-Americans resided east of the mill, the Hispanics were located across the tracks from them and the Indians lived on the west edge of town.

The Negro quarter and Hispanic quarter each had its own elementary school, church and cafe. From the early

Downtown McNary at an earlier time

years into the 1950s, Negro teenagers had to go to Flagstaff or Phoenix to attend high school.

In the 1970s, fire burned down the mill. The Apache Tribe refused to extend the lease to Southwest Forest Industries; and the lumber operation shut down and workers moved away. The Apache Tribe, in the meantime, had established its own sawmills on the reservation—Fort Apache Timber Company (FATCO) at Whiteriver and Cibecue.

Today, McNary is a sleepy Indian town. Just a ghost of itself. Only a small grocery store and post office remain, along with a couple of churches, an elementary school, Headstart center and community-branch library.

During tourist season, you can buy Indian fry bread out of a makeshift building, and a local resident plants a sign along the road advertising "worms" for sale.

Schools

The first school in the area opened in 1891 in Woodland, about three miles southwest of Pinetop village. Maud A. Judson taught the 20 students—11 girls and nine boys. The last names of the children were: Hansen, West, Lewis, Elsworth, Amos and what appears on the fancy handwritten register as "Buzan."

Hans Hansen, Ezra West and Sanford Jacques built a one-room log cabin school in 1893. Children from Pinetop attended the school in the early years.

However, in 1894, Pinetop provided its own school in Eph Penrod's home. Mr. Hollister taught this first group of students: Mac, Ralph and Cynthia Penrod; Della, Len and Lon Adams; Albert and Lee Carson; Belle, Cora, Lillie and Charlie Cooley; and Abe and C.D. (Dick) Amos.

Some of these students were not exactly young. Ralph Penrod was born in 1872, so he would have been 22 years old. Belle Cooley also was born in 1872. Her half-sister, Lillie, was about 18. (Their father, Corydon E. Cooley, had two Apache wives at the same time.) Romance must have blossomed in school. Abe Amos and Belle Cooley married that same year—1894.

In the summer of 1894, Pinetop folk built a one-room, log schoolhouse west of the William Penrod home. It is likely that William Penrod donated the land for the school. Mr. Kinter became the first teacher in this new building, which stood until 1923/24.

Horace Hansen (son of John Heber Hansen who helped colonize Lakeside) wrote that the Pinetop school had a large stove in the middle of the room to provide warmth during the winter months.

A new two-room frame structure took the place of the old school and a Miss Green, who came here from the Eastern U.S., taught in this school for many years. Edna Penrod began teaching in this two-room schoolhouse. Before she retired, she taught three generations of students.

Martin Penrod, grandson of William Penrod, recalled in his memoirs that another Penrod—Hattie—also at one time taught in the Pinetop school.

"Hattie caught Dan Adair and me throwing a sack of Bull Durham across the room to one another, the papers flew all across the floor and she came back with a ruler and broke it over Dan's head. She always whipped us with a ruler for anything we'd do. Damn she was a 'mean' teacher."

When enrollment in all eight grades reached a total of 40 children, another teacher, Alice Buell, became the school's second teacher. She had been living with her family in Lakeside, and she moved to Pinetop in the Fall of 1942 to assist Mrs. Penrod.

When Mrs. Penrod retired in 1954, Mr. Campbell became the head teacher, followed by Sam Jones. Mrs. Buell continued to teach the first four grades. Robert Overacker later became the third teacher in the Pinetop school.

In 1957, Pinetop voters unanimously approved a bond election to build a new school for $29,000. The U.S. Forest Service held a special levy and raised an additional $3,900.

The Navajo County supervisors collected additional fees and contributed $6,000.

Still, more money was needed. That's when community residents rolled up their sleeves and went to work. Logging crews donated their time to cut down allotted free trees in the forest. A man donated a truck to haul the logs to the mill and they were made into lumber free-of-charge. Others helped in the actual construction of the school.

When completed, authorities valued the school at $54,000, but the actual cost to taxpayers totaled only $29,290. The new school included two classrooms, a multi-purpose room, an office, storage rooms and restrooms.

Meanwhile, in Lakeside, the first school began in 1906/07 in Niels Hansen's house, with Miss Lucille Foster as teacher. Thirteen children from three families attended classes. They had books, slates and some paper and pencils to use. Several months later, workers converted a bunkhouse on the Hansen property into a schoolhouse. Miss Foster lived in a small bedroom in the Hansen house, where she boarded with the family. She received $35 a month.

Euphie Jones taught in 1908-09, followed by Pearl Potter and her sister Ruby Potter. The school moved to Charles Rhoton's store, which provided more space, but all classes still met in only one room.

In 1915, the town built its first major school building. Four years later, Lakeside High School opened with 13 freshmen and sophomore students, including four from Pinetop. About this time Wallace H. Larson moved to Lakeside and spent a long tenure teaching and being the principal of the school.

Pinetop never built a high school. When the company town of McNary began in the 1920s and a high school opened, Pinetop teens abandoned Lakeside High School and traveled an extra three miles or more to the McNary school.

McNary became the largest town in the region and offered more to Pinetop youth than Lakeside did. People in Lakeside contend that its high school just couldn't handle the growing high school population from Pinetop. Actually, since many viewed Lakeside as more of a bedroom community, a closer attachment became evident between residents of McNary and Pinetop. Both places combined offered more shopping and entertainment than Lakeside did. And Lakeside residents also traveled to Pinetop and McNary for shopping, dining and entertainment amenities.

However, in the early 1960s, it became evident that the borders between Pinetop and Lakeside were closing. Once a distinct three miles apart, new houses and businesses crept into the area between the two communities. Both Pinetop and Lakeside at the time were unincorporated and under Navajo County jurisdiction.

A public vote decided that the Pinetop and Lakeside school districts should merge, which eventually would become the four Blue Ridge schools—elementary, middle, junior high and high school.

In 1964, Lakeside High School became the "Pinetop-Lakeside High School," and Pinetop teens began attending there instead of McNary.

"Development of attractive home sites lying between the business districts of Lakeside and Pinetop promise to merge the two communities within a few years," according to a survey conducted by the College of Education at Arizona State University in June 1963.

"Another factor which virtually insures this merging process (of Lakeside and Pinetop school districts) is the acquiring of 73 acres from the U.S. Forest Service for the building sites of schools."

The survey noted that on April 25, 1963, a total of 257 elementary (grades 1-8) pupils and 106 high school students attended Lakeside schools and that 135 pupils attended the Pinetop elementary school.

The ASU survey listed these distinctions and comparisons between the Lakeside and Pinetop schools:

• Neither school had hot tables to keep food warm while serving and were limited in preparation by lack of sufficient oven space.

• Lakeside hot water supply was inadequate in as much as the 100-gallon electric water heater supplied hot water for restrooms as well as the kitchen.

• The sound conditioning at Lakeside cafeteria was adequate but was not at Pinetop due to reverberation from a wood-paneled ceiling.

• Cold storage facilities were not adequate at Lakeside but were sufficient at Pinetop.

• Lakeside had six tables which seat 60 elementary pupils in crowded conditions. Pinetop had 12 tables in an eating area of adequate size.

• Lakeside and Pinetop charged 25 cents a meal per pupil for a Type 'A' lunch. Lakeside charged the faculty 35 cents per meal while Pinetop charged 30 cents. Teachers collected the lunch money in each school.

• In 1962/63, there were a total of 19 teachers at both schools (Lakeside grades 1-12 and Pinetop 1-8).

• Lakeside school (both elementary and high school) was on about four acres. It "is fenced for safety of children and protection of lawn from roaming cattle."

• Pinetop Elementary School was on two acres and located half-block off the main highway. "The cinder-covered playground is unsatisfactory."

• "The Pinetop Elementary School consisted of two buildings resting on the site and one building that was either sold or donated to a church and later reconverted to school use. This old building does not rest on school property therefore the ownership might be questioned."

• The Pinetop school enrollment grew at a faster pace than the Lakeside enrollment. Lakeside had increased 50 per cent in five years (169 pupils in 1957/58 to 257 in 1962/

63) whereas Pinetop membership increased 150 per cent (52 in 1957/58 to 136 in 1962/63).

The survey noted that the designated Blue Ridge (named for the ridge near the two towns) "is one of the most beautiful high school sites in the state of Arizona."

The Blue Ridge High School became the first of the four schools completed on the new campus. The class of 1966 met first on the new location, followed by the elementary school in 1974. The middle and junior high schools later moved on campus. The high school expanded facilities in 1986. Today, the Blue Ridge Unified School District serves 2,300 students in the four schools. The size of the district is the smallest in Navajo County, encompassing 65 square miles.

The old Lakeside school buildings now house the Pinetop-Lakeside town offices and court.

Through the years, Blue Ridge Yellow Jackets football teams won several high school division state championships. Other sport teams have won state titles, too.

The school mascot wasn't always the Yellow Jackets.

"For many years, Lakeside High School's mascot was 'The Apaches,'" according to *Memories of Lakeside School 1906-1963*, a booklet compiled by the school alumnae. "Since we played various Indian reservation teams, especially Whiteriver, there was much confusion at the ball games.

"Every time our cheerleaders lead a cheer for the Lakeside Apaches all the Apache spectators on the opposing team would stand up and cheer!

"Therefore, in the year 1956-1957, the school voted to change the name. We became known as the 'Yellow Jackets,' the idea being that though we were rather small, as a team we carried a strong, deadly sting! Our school colors have always been purple and gold."

The Mountain Lights Up

The dominant electrical utility in the White Mountains is Navopache Electric Cooperative. It began by acquiring various community and independent electrical systems both on and off the Fort Apache Indian Reservation. Some of these systems were quite primitive. These acquisitions and the development of Navopache were mostly federally funded through the New Deal's Rural Electrification Administration (REA).

But it wasn't easy to get REA loans. According to Leah S. Glaser, in her doctorial dissertation on Arizona's rural electrification, some of the early problems in the White Mountains were poor economic status of Navajo and Apache counties, low population density, red tape dealing with Indian and U.S. Forest agencies and the generally rough terrain in the area.

It was evident from the beginning that large utility companies would not invest in this rural area because of the sparse population.

"Changes in economic income, a future promise of low-cost power from the Colorado River, and improvements in communication and transportation diminished these obstacles," Glaser observed.

From 1930 to 1950, the U.S. Census Bureau considered about 80 per cent of Navajo County and all of Apache County as rural. When the first settlers arrived in the White Mountains, they used candles for light and the fireplace for cooking and heating. After the railroad came to the area in the 1890s, people abandoned the home-made candles and bought the more readily available kerosene lamps. A few people upgraded to gas lamps they ordered from mailorder catalogs. Other homes acquired pot-bellied heaters that burned faster and produced greater heat than an ordinary fireplace or wood stove.

Then, in small communities, someone would build a small generating unit and maybe even hook a line through tree tops to his neighbor's homes.

This happened in Lakeside. Mainly in the early 1930s, there were various attempts to generate power to homes using both diesel and water-churning power.

Raymond Johnson, chairman of the history committee for the Pinetop-Lakeside Historical Society, reported that his father, Abe Johnson, was successful in his attempt to build the first water-powered, electric-light plant on a Lakeside creek. He and a co-worker ran wires into town. Although Abe Johnson didn't have experience or knowledge on how to construct a generating plant, he obtained plans and materials and diligently went to work to bring electricity to town.

"When the flood gates were opened and the water began spinning paddle wheels, low and behold, Lakeside lit up like a Christmas tree," said Raymond Johnson. "(Abe) Johnson was amazed and astounded that it actually worked."

A man by the last name of Symes decided to dam up a creek leading to Rainbow Lake. The cement dam enclosed a small, rocky valley, and the moving water turned a large waterwheel, possibly 10-feet high, producing hydro-electric power. Symes reduced the voltage from 2,300 to 110 volts and electrical wires were strung on poles to town.

The plant generated enough electrical power for two hours per night and one day each week.

This system worked for almost four years, until Symes went broke and the power plant closed. M.L. Fish moved the waterwheel and generator to a new site in 1936. The Fish family then ran a diesel-power electric plant for several years. The dam remained intact for a while, then the Arizona Game and Fish Department dynamited part of it to allow Rainbow Lake's trout to swim upstream to spawn.

Lawrence Lee, a self-taught electrician, ran Lakeside's first four-cylinder diesel engine light plant from 5 a.m. until 9 p.m. daily. At closing time, Lee would "blink" the electricity twice to warn his "customers" that he was about to shut off the generator.

When the plant shut down at night, many families lit gaslights. They were astounded that the gaslight only dimly illuminated the room compared to the brilliance of an electric bulb.

Meanwhile, while White Mountain communities were trying to generate electrical power, the same thing was happening on the Fort Apache Indian Reservation.

In 1922, Congress decommissioned Fort Apache as a military post. A year later, the Bureau of Indian Affairs established a boarding school at the fort. It accommodated 250 Indian students, ironically, mostly Navajo. The fort was in disrepair, but improvements were made, including a newly-built diesel, electrical-power plant.

In Whiteriver, capital of the White Mountain Apache Tribe, a hydroelectric plant on the White River supplied power to businesses, homes, schools, hospitals and Christian missions.

Twenty miles away at McNary, a company lumber town leased from the tribe, sawdust and wood scraps were heaped into burners to fuel large turbines that churned out electrical power for the mill, manufacturing plant and parts of the town. The power plant was the largest generating plant in the White Mountains for decades.

"Increasingly, the generating equipment at towns like Whiteriver, Lakeside and Holbrook were often unreliable and operators found it more difficult to meet their system's expanding needs and to pay operating expenses at the same time," writes Glaser in her report.

Someone looked at the possibility of building a hydroelectric plant on the Little Colorado River, but it was determined that the project would be too expensive.

Many ideas to "electrify" homes throughout the White Mountains were tossed around, but it seemed the only solution would be REA loans.

"Different communities in southern Apache and Navajo counties had made several early, but failed, attempts to secure REA loan money," Glaser noted.

Momentum for REA loans increased after World War II. Prospects for more people moving to the area and businesses opening up were evident. The Forest Service issued additional leases for summer cottages.

People in the White Mountains said they would use more appliances if more reliable and affordable electrical power became available.

In 1946, a group of Lakeside people formed Navopache Electric Cooperative, an outgrowth of White Mountain Electric Cooperative formed 10 years earlier. WMEC had failed when World War II broke out because needed line materials went into the war effort.

With a $62,000 loan from REA, Navopache bought a small diesel-powered plant and constructed a power line from Lakeside to McNary. The co-op bought wholesale energy from McNary's power source. It's first customers were in Pinetop and Lakeside communities. By 1948, Navopache had 1,025 members, or customers.

In 1958, Navopache acquired the Whiteriver-Fort Apache distribution system, which consisted of both hydroelectric and diesel-powered plants, from the Bureau of Indian Affairs (BIA).

Through the years, Navopache expanded its coverage in all directions, including into New Mexico and to remote areas such as Big Lake, Young, Blue and Hannagan Meadow.

Electric crews had to work in extremely rough terrain, including clearing easements in malapai, or volcanic, rock. The company rented helicopters to set poles.

"Three different contractors, who had experience building REA power lines in places like Texas and the Midwest, severely underestimated the Eastern Arizona landscape and went bankrupt trying to negotiate the landscape between Springerville and Reserve, New Mexico," Glaser said.

Navopache had problems with the U.S. Forest Service, which refused to grant easements across forest lands where a power line might interfere with buildings, scenic views or watersheds.

The Sitgreaves National Forest had rudimentary telephone lines strung on treetops across valley floors to connect ranger buildings. A power line had to run at least a quarter-mile away from the phone line in order to avoid interference. This forced Navopache to string lines onto the sides of hills or canyon walls, making construction and maintenance exceedingly difficult and expensive.

Through plain grit, Navopache Electric has now grown to 33,818 active accounts; 229 miles of transmission lines and 2,845 miles of distribution lines over an area of 10,000 square miles.

It services customers in Navajo, Apache, Gila and Greenlee counties in Arizona and Catron County in New Mexico. Its assets are $57.6 million.

Wayne Retzlaff, general manager of Navopache Electric since 1990, said the non-profit company has been granted about 20 REA loans since Navopache started in 1946. It has had its ups and downs through the years. Underground cable that was supposed to last 30 years had to be replaced after 10 years. Gophers and moisture taunting the 14,000 volts trying to get out of the cables were the culprits.

During the 2002 Rodeo-Chediski fire, the company "lost only 60 poles." A new computer system now allows a switch to be turned on or off to correct a problem 120 miles away. Before, a lineman had to be sent to check out the problem.

In a 1996 newsletter on the co-op's 50th anniversary, an article concluded:

"Navopache Electric Cooperative was founded on the principle of improving the rural way of life for the communities we serve, and we have accomplished this by way of persistence in the wake of adversity. This pioneering spirit remains strong and acts as the undercurrent which drives us with confidence into the headwind of the future."

Navopache Electric Cooperative workers install and maintain power lines that serve nearly 34,000 customers

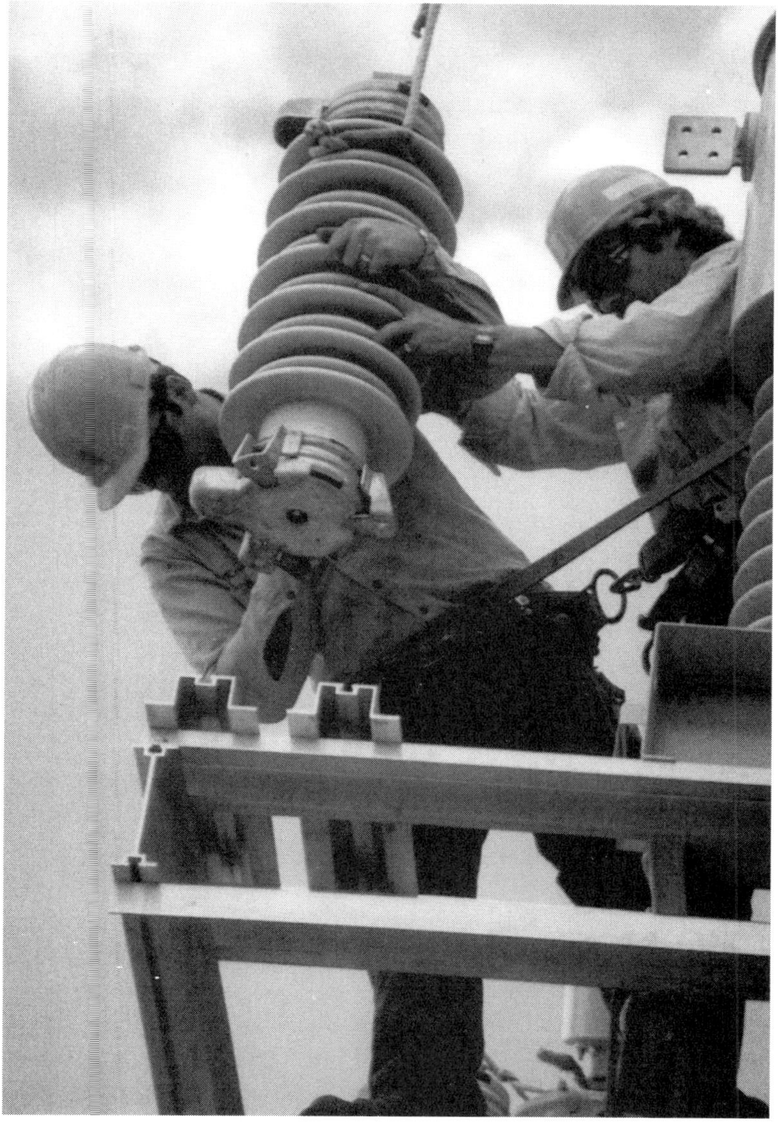

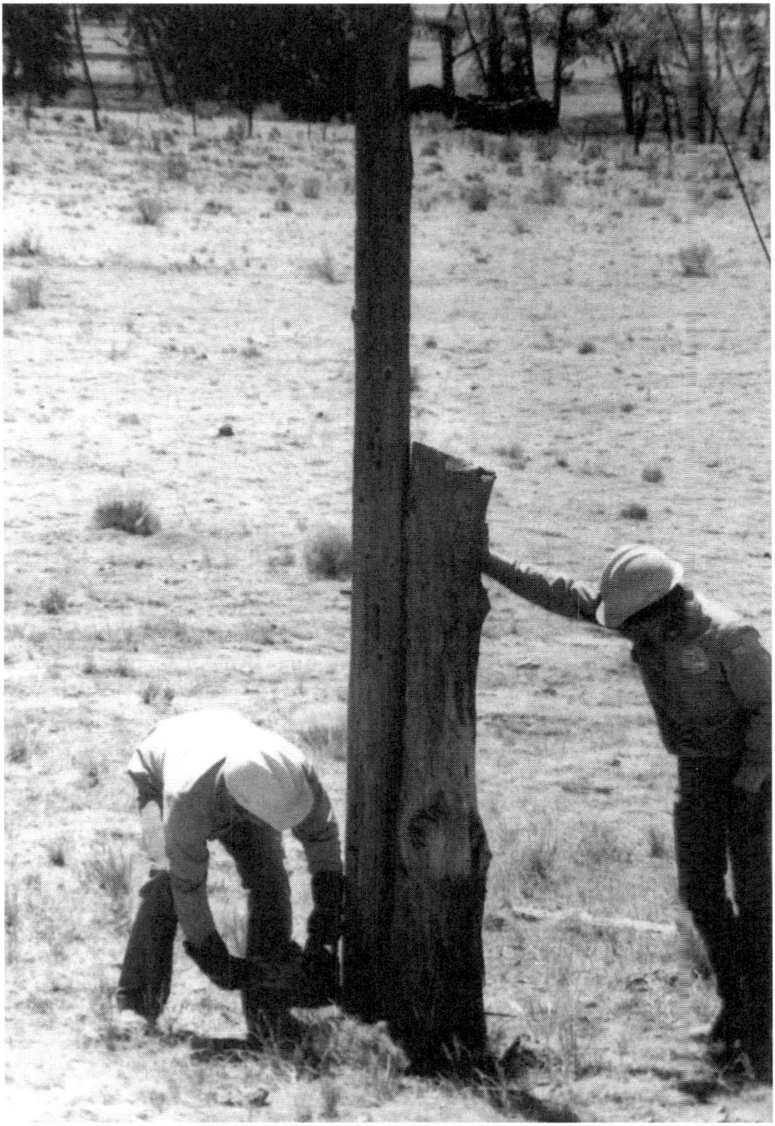

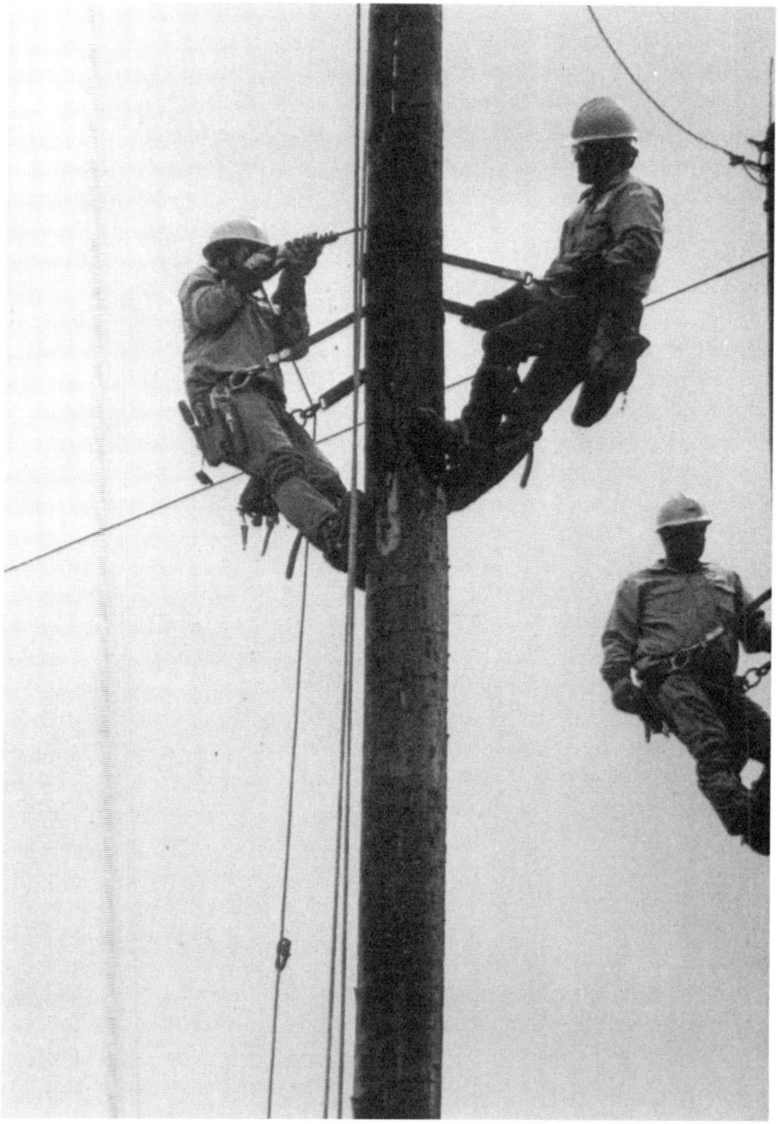

Pinetop on the Move

Pinetop never was a saintly settlement. After all, its first settler opened a saloon, and one of Mormon Patriarch William Penrod's sons also ran a bar. And Pinetop's Dew Drop Inn was notorious for fights, stabbings and a killing or two. During Prohibition, a Pinetop cafe sold moonshine, and, later, the town's saloons housed illegal slot machines. In the 1950s Pinetop had its own red-light district—a brothel in the back of a bar, which now is part of the parking lot of Pinetop's First Baptist Church. Pinetop had a jail; Lakeside didn't.

Through the years, some saints in Pinetop traveled on Sundays down the road to attend services at its saintly, sister-settlement of Lakeside. Lakeside was colonized by Mormons; Pinetop wasn't. Pinetop Mormons were part of the Show Low Ward for 28 years, followed by 66 more years as part of the Lakeside Ward. In 1978, Pinetop's LDS membership grew enough to merit having its own ward.

Although Pinetop and Lakeside were only separated by three miles, their reputations were worlds apart.

Raymond Lee smiles when he recounts his earliest memories of Pinetop back in the 1940s and 50s.

People around here referred to Pinetop as "Winetop" or even "Bottletop," because of all the establishments that had liquor licenses, said Lee, born in 1939 and a resident of Lakeside most of his life.

People said there were just as many liquor licenses in Pinetop as there were families, Lee added.

Pinetop's location catered to the drinking, dining and dancing crowds. Liquor could not be sold on the Indian reservation, which Pinetop borders, and, in the beginning, troops from Fort Apache stopped in town for their liquid refreshments. After the fort closed in 1922, McNary blossomed as a sawmill town on the reservation and residents traveled to Pinetop, their nearest booze-selling town. McNary, which flourished from the 1920s through the early 70s, boasted of being the largest town in the area.

Pinetop learned early that to survive economically it must cater mainly to visitors, just as it does today, accommodating tourists and summer residents.

Lee said that when he was a lad in the early 1950s, telephones were scarce in the area. Lakeside had them, but Pinetop didn't. He would hop on his bicycle at Lakeside's telephone office and pedal three miles on the two-way road to deliver phone messages to Pinetop residents. He estimated that in the mid-50s Pinetop had about 24 families and Lakeside had twice as many.

But that would change. Pinetop would hit paydirt when developers converted vast amounts of pine-encrusted land for subdivisions and country-club living. Many of these houses became second homes for desert-weary Phoenix and Tucson residents. In the second half of the 20th Century, Pinetop would boast of having three golf courses, two private and one public. That also meant hundreds of homes scattered around these courses.

Frank Crosby, son-in-law of Charlie Clark, and a few others became the sparkplug to change Pinetop from "Winetop" to one of the most prestigious resort towns in Arizona, if not the Southwest.

Raymond Lee

Besides running Charlie Clark's for a few years, Crosby also became involved in banking and real estate businesses and he served in the state legislature and senate for a short time. Crosby said he developed Pinetop Hills, the first major housing development in Pinetop.

"It really kicked Pinetop off and got it started," he said. "It got me started, too."

Crosby said he struck a 200-acre land exchange deal with the U.S. Forest Service. Part of the land he developed had previously been a "huge garbage dump" along an abandoned road.

Crosby also was instrumental in the development of White Mountain Country Club and Pinetop Country Club, where homes costing $400,000 and more are not uncommon.

In the early 1950s, Lakeside District Manager Nelson Bernard approached Crosby about starting White Mountain Country Club on the site of the old Civilian Conservation Corps (CCC) camp next to the Indian reservation.

Bernard's father was a golf pro back in the East somewhere, Crosby said. With help from some Phoenix investors, the White Mountain Summer Homes and golf course help put Pinetop on the map.

"When it took off I didn't know a golf ball from a roll of toilet paper," Crosby said. "They got me enthused about it and I worked with the board over there and helped build it."

Crosby also was instrumental in the starting of Pinetop Country Club.

About 1960, Southwest Forest Industries, which operated the sawmill in McNary, acquired 1,196 acres that was once part of Sitgreaves National Forest. Southwest Forest intended to move its McNary lumber operations onto that land in Pinetop. Southwest held the land for a few years, then abandoned its plans, putting the entire property up for sale.

Crosby, Bob Fernandez and Glen L. Jones formed a partnership in 1964 and obtained an option to purchase this acreage.

At first, before Crosby came aboard, the plan focused on putting in a few roads and selling off five-acre sites. Crosby said he balked at this suggestion, saying "you will have a whole lot of chicken ranches there."

He suggested subdividing the area and putting in a golf course. Crosby called Gray Madison, a Phoenix golfer who also worked on the White Mountain Country Club Golf Course, and asked if he would look at the land.

"We walked around the land," Crosby said. "He went back to Phoenix and he called me the next day or two and said, I've been working on the development and we can't find water. If the land you are interested in you can show me water, I'll come in and join you and we will see if we can develop it.'"

Crosby said he hired a "well witcher" who walked around with his witching sticks and he found a place to drill a well.

"Three of us kicked in more money and got a well drilled up there," Crosby said. He (well witcher) got water. I called Gray and Gray came up and we got some other people interested in it."

The limited partnership developed the land, formed a country club and sold off properties.

Later, Pinetop's third country club—Pinetop Lakes Golf & Country Club—adjacent to Pinetop Country Club was formed. It's golf course is open to the public, whereas the White Mountain and Pinetop country clubs are private.

And Crosby's leadership role in developing land in Pinetop has not gone unnoticed. A street is named after him—Crosby Road. "I guess the surveyors ran out of names," he said. "I'm the only founder (of Pinetop Country Club) that is still around."

Golfers at Pinetop Country Club

Others who have had a role in Pinetop-Lakeside's developing history also are honored. There is an Alchesay Drive; Madison Lane; Penrod Lane; Adair Drive; Cooley Lane; Hall Lane; Jackson Lane; John L. Fish Lane; Johnson Street; Larson Road; Lee's Drive; McCoy Drive; McNeill Street; Niels Hansen Drive; Peterson Drive; Phipps Drive; Rhoton Lane; Scott's Drive and Stephens Drive. And, to cover all bases, making sure no pioneer is forgotten, there is "Settlers Lane."

But not everyone was happy with all the development in Pinetop. Fernandez regretted what he did to the mountain and he moved to California, said Jo Baeza, Pinetop resident and newspaper reporter.

Along with his work as one of the developers of Pinetop Country Club, Fernandez also ran bulldozers into the forest and carved out such places as Moon Ridge subdivision and Ponderosa RV Resort.

He felt responsible for helping to "spoil" the mountain, said Baeza, who was Fernandez's secretary for nearly two years.

Baeza, who has lived in the area for more than 50 years, agreed with her former boss and she, too, regretted that Pinetop had sprawled the way it did. This boom came in the 1970s, she said.

"I liked it back in the 60s when it was a little mountain town," she said. "Before, everyone helped each other out. Everyone was poor. You could drink water in any stream."

The Two Shall Become One

"Save the trees" was the cry after the twin communities of Pinetop and Lakeside incorporated as one village in 1984. One of the first orders of business of the new town council was to pass an ordinance restricting the cutting of pine trees of more than 6 inches in diameter.

Also, it virtually put a lock-box on the chainsaw and axe in town. No more than five trees could be removed from a development lot and no more than two from any other lot in a one-year period, unless approved in a site or plot plan.

In some cases, no trees will be allowed to be cut down, because all the sites will be inspected personally by town officials, said Kevin Dunlap, town manager, who was quoted in the March 11, 1985 issue of *The Arizona Republic*.

"I wouldn't go as far as to say that we are in the forefront of the environmental movement, but we are adopting strong planning and zoning techniques."

Before incorporation, residents complained about all the trees that were cut down along State Route 260 to allow for businesses to sprout up. This destroyed the beauty of a forest setting, they argued. The new town council agreed.

Now, fast forward 20 years. In 2003, the Pinetop-Lakeside town council turned about-face and passed an ordinance encouraging residents to thin out trees on their properties. What a difference 20 years make!

Because of the Rodeo-Chediski fire that destroyed hundreds of White Mountain homes in 2002 west of Pinetop-Lakeside, reality set in. The area is really a tinder box ready for a fiery explosion.

The drought, and the fact that there are just too many trees on lots or in the forest, is the reason for the change of attitude. The law forbidding cutting trees over 6 inches in diameter made the problem the town has now a lot worse. These overpopulated trees fight for whatever little moisture they can find in the ground and thus become stressed. Bark beetles like this because these weakened trees are prime targets. Beetles won't attack a healthy tree.

Bark beetles are not only killing trees in Pinetop-Lakeside, but have caused even more devastation in other parts of Arizona.

This new ordinance gives homeowners two years to remove all flammable forest materials within 10 feet of homes, followed by another two years for the removal of such fire-hazardous debris 30 feet out and two additional years to thin land within 100 feet of homes.

In the meantime, the town council has its fingers crossed that (a) the drought will end soon and (b) a devastating fire won't sweep into the town, like the one that destroyed most of Sumerhaven on Mount Lemmon near Tucson in 2003. It can't do anything about the former, but it believes it has a handle on the latter.

The Lakeside Ranger District, which borders part of Pinetop-Lakeside, completed 440 acres of forest thinning north of town, primarily near the area of Pinetop Springs in the Fall of 2003, as well as starting to remove combustible debris in the Woodland Lake Park Tract. Thinning also has started around Woodland Lake, which the town uses under a Forest Service Special Use Permit for picnic ramadas, sports fields, a walking trail and a fishing and boating lake.

Just before incorporation in 1984, many in the state classified the two communities as one. A commercial strip connected the towns and it was hard for the visitor to determine where the boundary was between Pinetop and Lakeside.

The *Pinetop-Lakeside News* covered events in both towns. The two school districts joined together as one in the 1960s. In 1975, a group of 14 University of Arizona students conducted a survey of Pinetop-Lakeside for the Arizona Office of Economic Planning and Development. It determined that there were a total of 246 businesses in the two communities. There was no distinction as to whether a firm was in Pinetop or Lakeside.

"The economy of the area reflects a pattern common to resort communities," the survey said. "Over 70 percent of the firms are in the retail trade and services sectors."

The 1975 survey also noted that over 70 percent of the businesses that gave data on current ownership were established after 1970, indicating a proliferation of new businesses and/or turnover of existing ones.

This "one-town" mindset almost necessitated that the two villages incorporate and become one.

But it was a hard sell. In 1980, the issue of incorporation was brought before the voters, and it was turned down by a 2-1 ratio.

Another attempt to incorporate was made three years later. Proponents estimated that 666 registered voters lived in the two towns. They accumulated 523 signatures, seemingly enough to incorporate. State law required valid signatures of two-thirds of the registered voters in an area for incorporation.

The day before the deadline to submit the petitions, however, Navajo County officials determined that 708 signatures would be needed because there were 1,063 voters in the proposed incorporated area.

"We didn't have enough time to recover," said Mary Ellen Bittorf, who spearheaded both the 1980 drive and this one. "They didn't compile their list until the last minute, and we were left out in the cold."

Undaunted, Bittorf and other proponents went back to the 1980 tactic calling for the 1984 election. Only 10 percent of the voters in the area were needed to ask for an election.

"If people sit on their duffs, they'll pass this thing," said Buck Goar in an *Arizona Republic* article Feb. 21, 1984. He was manager of the Ponderosa Water Co. and president of the Pinetop Water Co. He predicted the proposal would be turned down again.

"I think people will take a close look at the costs. I see it as just another governmental agency. I feel we're pretty damned overgoverned already."

However, more than enough signatures were gotten and the election was scheduled for July 24, 1984.

The townspeople of both communities debated the issue among themselves. There were heated arguments.

The *Pinetop-Lakeside News* in an editorial favored incorporation but warned that the new council must be able to work at a "madman's pace," not the often typical "mountain pace."

An advertisement in the same July 19 issue asked voters if they wanted a local government or 50-mile trips to Holbrook (county seat) for action or to be heard. It also contended there should be local control over building and zoning, instead of letting things be run by those who live in other parts of the county.

Residents in the proposed 5-square mile area of Pinetop and Lakeside went to the poll. Incorporation was approved by a 290 to 264 margin.

Those living within the new town's boundary who wanted to serve on the first council sent applications to the county board of supervisors. Residents took a straw vote of the applicants, and the supervisors appointed the top seven to serve until an election could be held the following year.

The first council members were attorney Jay Natoli, who was voted mayor by other council members, Bittorf, Duane Walker, Rich Mullins, B.C. Irwin, Larry Hudson and Jane Chavez.

The members first met at a workshop session Aug. 30, 1984. Two people from the League of Arizona Cities and Towns were present to advise these neophytes on how to set up and run a town.

The first council meeting open to the public would be held a few hours later. Natoli suggested the Pledge of Allegiance be recited to open the meetings. Walker recommended a prayer also be given.

"A motion was made by Walker to open the meeting with the Pledge of Allegiance followed by a prayer," the minutes read. "Larry Hudson seconded the motion. Six of the council were in favor of the motion, one was against."

The 7 p.m. meeting was opened by the Pledge, followed by a prayer by Walker. This meeting was held in a room at a Blue Ridge school. The town at this point had no building of its own (it would later take over the old Lakeside School) and soon the council members had to practice "back room" politics. That's because at the Sept 6 meeting the council announced the next meetings will move "to the back room at the First Interstate Bank."

At a work session Sept. 13 about possible annexation, the minutes showed that "Walker felt that we ought to go right down the highway to the Show Low limits taking 200 feet on each side and not add anymore road expense." The council didn't buy the idea.

On Sept. 27, the council, which then rented space to conduct the town's business, voted to get up to four phones and "the largest post office box available as soon as possible."

At an October meeting, records showed the town owed $902 for the first and last month's rent on office space. Blue Ridge School District wanted payment of $17.91 for "use of the multi-purpose room." The post office box drawer and two keys cost $19. Also, the State of Arizona sent Pinetop-Lakeside a bill for $90 to subscribe to the State Purchase Agreement. Next on the agenda: a $283 bill for meals the council members ate between work sessions and public meetings; $600 for a typewriter from Larson Memorial Public Library; and $17.20 to C&E Office Supply for, obviously, office supplies.

Also in October, the council hired Leslee Wessel as secretary at $5.25 per hour with nine paid holidays. She was the town's first employee. Through the years, she advanced to town clerk and assistant personnel director.

These were the first few weeks of the new town. It got more complicated as the years went by. A police department was established; an animal control officer hired; a parks department developed; and soon the town was off and running with other amenities at a "madman's pace."

The *White Mountain Independent* in a Feb. 6, 2004, editorial said the town will spend just over $3.17 million in 2004 on general fund items such as police, magistrate court, engineering, economic development, planning and zoning and maintaining the Lakeside cemetery. The town also will spend $240,500 to advertise and promote itself to tourists. Within the borders of Pinetop-Lakeside there are about $53,248,702 worth of property. This figure would be higher, but the three country club areas (White Mountain, Pinetop and Pinetop Lakes) are in the county, not in town.

Even with the drought and possible wildfire danger, construction in Pinetop-Lakeside broke records in 2003. The *White Mountain Independent* reported on March 16, 2004, that both commercial and residential building surpassed previous records set in 2001. The valuation of all permits in 2003 was $17.562 million, or about $4.3 million more than the 2001 record. Residential construction valuation outnumbered commercial about 3 to 1.

Although officially the town is called Pinetop-Lakeside, practically all of the residents refer to themselves as residents of either Pinetop or Lakeside. There is a Pinetop Post Office and a Lakeside Post Office, not a Pinetop-Lakeside post office. And there is a Pinetop Fire Department and a Lakeside Fire Department (neither is under town control but are separate fire districts).

Pinetop often gets top billing around the state. On the weather map on Phoenix's Channel 3's "Good Morning Arizona," the town is simply listed as Pinetop. In *The Arizona Republic's* Oct. 16, 2003, edition, a story noted that there are 88 incorporated towns and cities in Arizona. In the 1980s, eleven communities were incorporated. Pinetop was one of them, not "Pinetop-Lakeside."

Safeway on State Route 260 is the dividing line between Pinetop and Lakeside. However, Pinetop Office Supply store is clearly in Lakeside and Lakeside Cinema is just over the line in Pinetop. The Navajo County Sheriff's branch office is in the incorporated area, not the county. And the Lakeside Cemetery is in the county, not the town. But the town maintains it.

And, it seems, as the area grows, more confusion will abound in Pinetop and Lakeside, or, should we say officially, "Pinetop-Lakeside."

Pinetop People

At age 5, Jo Baeza became enchanted with the wild west and the cowboy life. She gulped down Ralston hot cereal because it sponsored the Tom Mix radio show. She followed the Lone Ranger and Tonto in the comic strips, and on Saturdays looked forward attending Gene Autry's movies.

At this young age, the Minnesota youngster would lie in bed, wheezing because of her asthma, and promised herself that some day she would be strong and healthy. She would ride horses and walk in clean, sunlit air.

"When I grow up, if I ever do, I shall go to Arizona and be a cowboy," Jo thought to herself. She records all this in her autobiographical book, *Ranch Wife*.

Her journey was long and circuitous, and after graduation from Stanford University with a year of study at the University of Nottingham in England, she came back to her parents home in Holbrook. They had moved there earlier from Minnesota.

And it was there in the high grassland plateau she fell in love with Cooney Jeffers, a local rancher. They married and Jo lived out her childhood dream of being a "cowboy."

She did plenty of cookin' in the kitchen, but she often got up early to do the work her male counterparts did—herd cattle, help at branding time, milk a cow, help dig out a cow stuck in mud and, while alone, pulled out a calf that was stuck in his mother's uterus.

This life on the ranch lasted a few years and, when the marriage ended, Jo moved to Pinetop in 1964. Her dad objected, saying there was no work there. He was nearly right. The only job in town was $50 a week working as a secretary to real estate developer Bob Fernandez, Jo said in a 2004 interview.

Why Pinetop? "I just loved the mountains," she said. Jo first visited Pinetop in 1950 as a teenager, after her family moved to Holbrook.

"There were two places to go out on a special night on the town," Jo said. "Harvey House in Winslow and Charlie Clark's. These were elegant places to eat."

At that time, Mabel Bowles owned much of Pinetop.

"She was a wild woman," Jo said. "She must have made her money in California. She came out and bought a lot of land. She thought it would be developed. She was the first (Pinetop) land broker. She saw the potential."

Jo said Bowles' granddaughter, Thelma Axline, told her that Pinetop's first settler, Johnny Phipps, was buried in the meadow east of Charlie Clark's. Axline also told Jo that three other graves of "bad guys" are in that same meadow near a dead tree.

"In the 50s there wasn't much of anything in Pinetop," Jo said, adding that there were only a few businesses around. "Pinetop was built on bootleggers," Jo said, noting that years ago abandoned stills could be found in the area.

But Pinetop in the 50s and when she moved there in the 60s was a place "to have fun," unlike Lakeside, which was a Mormon town without any bars, Jo said.

Jo remembers in those days climbing over the fence at Fred's Lake to ice skate in the winter. She and friends also ice skated on Billy Creek.

In 1966, Jo and J.P.S. Brown, a western author, married. Jo raised his two children, Bill, who was then 10, and Paula, 9.

"I had them for 10 years," Jo said. "My kids were raised like (kids were) 100 years ago. They rode horses and did outdoor stuff."

Jo wrote in a May 4, 2004 column in *White Mountain Independent* that there wasn't much to do in Pinetop during those years. The town dump, where Pine Lake is now, was the center of family entertainment. "When the bears came out of hibernation families drove up to the Pinetop dump at night and parked with their headlights on to watch the bears rummage through the dump."

And the dump was a great place for people, including Jo's children, to find "treasures."

Jo supplemented the family's income by operating a little gift shop, La Serrana, that sold upgrade Mexican imports and Indian arts and crafts. There was another gift shop in town, Patrol House, that handled European items. People from the country clubs patronized these gift shops, Jo said.

Jo's marriage with Brown ended in 1974 during the time she was very ill with Rocky Mountain Spotted Fever. She was unable to work for several years.

Once in a while, though, she would write magazine articles, some of which appeared in *Arizona Highways.*

One day while in Snowflake after getting treatment and looking very gaunt, a Mexican cowboy and singer, Luis Mario Baeza, walked past her and gawked.

"What happened to you?" Jo said he asked. Jo explained her serious illness.

"He saved my life," Jo said. "He helped me get better. I owe my life to him. He took care of me."

Jo Baeza

For five years, Jo and Luis were together as a married couple. He got a job on the Apache Railroad and when he came home after work he cooked and "made me eat," Jo said. He also made her take walks so she would get exercise and get her strength back.

The couple lived on an old ranch on the Mogollon Rim between Show Low and Heber.

"It was very remote and wild," Jo said. "There was no electricity or running water. It was very secluded and pretty much what I needed to get well."

The couple raised Arabian/mustang horses, and Luis broke horses for people.

In 1981 they went their separate ways and Jo moved back to Pinetop to start her career as a newspaper reporter with the *White Mountain Independent*. She was well versed in writing, having written her autographical book, *Ranch Wife*, and numerous magazine articles through the years.

"In 1981 two things happened to me," Jo said. "I became Catholic. I raised both of my kids in the Catholic Church and I made up my mind I will be single the rest of my life. I also started my newspaper business."

Through the years, Jo has written hundreds of historical stories on the area, people profiles and current news articles. She continues to freelance with magazine articles and she is in the process of writing a second book on a historical hotel her grandparents owned in Minnesota.

Jo has taught creative writing and English courses for 18 years at Northland Pioneer College. For 16 summers, she scanned the tops of trees while sitting in lookout towers on Lake, Springer, Juniper Ridge and Deer Springs mountains for the U.S. Forest Service.

"I always liked Pinetop," Jo said. "When I first moved up there people minded their own business. They didn't gossip. They were tough mountain people."

But if a need arose, neighbors and Pinetop friends were always around to help out, she said.

Jo said her parents couldn't quite understand why she stayed in this area, with her metropolitan background, demonstrated by her attending Stanford, outside San Francisco, and living in England.

"I told my parents I never would leave Navajo County. This is where my heart was and my stories are."

• • •

Sarah Mason received a frantic call from her mother, Dora Hunter, who lived around the corner on Rim Road adjacent to reservation forest land.

"There's a bear lying on top of my car and I have to go out and do errands," Dora told her daughter. Dora also called police.

The policeman who arrived in a patrol car wasn' sure what to do. He just turned on the whirling lights and let the siren scream, hoping to scare the bear away. It worked, sort of. The bear crawled off the car and sauntered away. The policeman left.

Dora had last minute things to do in the house before she ran out to do her errands. The bear had returned and was lying again on top of her car. This time Dora just waited and eventually the bear left.

Joe and Sarah Mason, who moved to Pinetop in 1972, have had numerous bear encounters through the years. They said they have seen them every summer near Pinetop Mountain where they live, except in recent years, since the Rodeo-Chediski fire. Because of the drought, the wild berries in the nearby forest are just not as plentiful.

One time Sarah heard noise around the trash container outside; she opened the door and saw a bear. She slammed the door shut and the bear ran away. Another time she opened the door and a huge bear was 15 feet away. He stood up, and Sarah yelled: "You can have anything you want." Sarah estimated the bear stood 8-feet tall.

Another time, Sarah was outside washing a picnic table when through the bushes a baby bear came walking toward her.

"I ran into the house," Sarah said. "I didn't see the mother but I knew she was around here."

Joe and Sarah and another couple were laughing and talking while walking in the middle of Rim Road, when all of a sudden a bear ran to the edge of the road and stopped. They were all startled, including the bear.

Once, while the couple was hiking on a road near their home, a car passed them and suddenly stopped directly in front of them. A huge bear was walking across the road just in front of the car.

"At first we thought to get in the car; we were real close to the bear," Sarah said.

Another time Joe and Sarah heard commotion on the next street. "One of the kids came by and said a bear was in a tree," Sarah said. Authorities shot the bear with a tranquilizer dart and put it in a cage and hauled it away.

Joe explained that bears were used to eating out of residents' garbage containers bringing bears into neighborhoods. Local authorities would put meat in a cage atop a trailer. When a bear ventured inside the door would close. A truck would then back up to hook onto the trailer, then the truck would cart off the bear.

The Masons tell one more story about bears. Their friends, Shirley and Kirk, lived in a trailer on Rim Road. Shirley heard something outside, so she raised the blinds and looked outside. A bear standing on its hind legs inches away peered at her from the other side of the window. Both became frightened.

"It was wet on both sides of the window," Sarah laughed.

"A mountain lion used to live up here," Joe said. Wild turkey, elk, javalina, raccoons, rattlesnakes and an assortment of squirrels, chipmunks and various birds have been seen near Pinetop Mountain.

Businesses in Pinetop changed often in the 70s and 80s, Joe and Sarah said. One popular place was Mr. C'zs. Local talent put on shows in a community theater on Woodland Lake Road. When storms knocked electricity out at Little Bears store, the owner handed out flashlights so customers could continue their shopping. Paul Bunyan's restaurant with sawdust floors served up delicious roast beef and pepper steak sandwiches. Joe Carter drove through Pinetop with his pickup truck loaded with 3-to 5-foot-tall blue spruce trees. He sold trees for $10 each and even planted it. If the tree died within a year Carter would replace it free of charge.

Joe and Sarah raised a son, Gary, in Pinetop. There were many families in 1975 with children living near Pinetop Mountain and at Hon-Dah homesites farther east on Rim Road. Sarah surveyed the area and came up with from 25 to 30 kids living in the area, but parents had to take turns driving the children to the country store on Highway 260 for the school bus. This was as much as three miles or more for some parents.

Sarah called the school and asked why they wouldn't send a school bus on Rim Road to pick up the kids. She was told that part of Rim Road was thought to be on the Indian reservation, and it would cost $300 to make a survey and for the matter to be settled.

The school refused to come up with the $300 so Sarah went to businesses in town to raise the necessary $300. The survey completed, Pinetop Mountain and Hon Dah families got their school bus.

• • •

Sue Penrod chuckles at a dog she used to own that climbed on top of its dog house. She looked out her kitchen window and there he was—looking down at her. That was after the blizzard of 1967, when seven feet of snow fell and the dog crawled on top of his snow-covered dog house.

Joe and Sarah Mason

Sue, a life-long resident of McNary and Pinetop, said the storm began with three or four days of rain and then it snowed constantly for days. "It never let up," she said. Her husband, Sonny, who worked at McNary, could not get home for three days.

The mill there caved in and he was plowing snow.

People were snowed in throughout the Mountain. Mailmen couldn't make their rounds and fresh vegetables and fruit couldn't be hauled into town. The roof of Pinetop's Wilbur's Market collapsed, but the fire department was able to keep the building secure enough and open for business.

Sue said that years ago winters had much more snowfall. But that began to change in the mid-1980s. It seemed that ever since then less and less snow fell each year ushering in the drought and extreme fire danger seasons.

During the 2002 Rodeo-Chediski fire, Sonny, assistant chief for the Pinetop Fire Department, stayed behind and Sue and her daughter, Karen, and grandson, Willy, evacuated to a relative's two-bedroom cabin in Greer. They traveled with two dogs, a cat that was scared of everyone, four pheasants, a cockatiel and two iguanas, one of which was five-feet long. Then someone in Greer injured a pigeon, probably with a slingshot, and their menagerie increased by one. They had to nurse the pigeon back to health.

Sue said living in Pinetop is just not the same, nor as much fun as it was decades ago, before the big housing boom. "Everyone knew everyone then," she said. Back in the 1960s the population of Pinetop was only about 300 or 400 people, she estimated.

She also has fond memories growing up in McNary. Her father, Bill Quick, ran the bowling alley and was considered the mayor of the town, while her mother, Grace, operated the boarding house/hotel. Sue grew up living in the hotel.

It was an old building and when she had slumber parties with her girlfriends they got scared because of stories that were told of the hotel being haunted. She has a picture of Sen. Barry Goldwater, who stayed at the hotel, with her father.

McNary was the hub of the whole White Mountains and the mill was the only industry, Sue said.

"The theater was so much fun especially at Christmas," she said. "We would sit in there and watch cartoons for two hours and then sacks of candy and fruit were brought on the stage. Santa Claus would show up and we'd get in line." Each child got a sack to take home.

Sue said that during the Yuletide season Christmas carols would be broadcast over the general store's loudspeakers and the music could be heard throughout town.

The town had wooden sidewalks and all the houses had flowers in their yards. She remembers when television first came to town. She and her friends would hurry from school to the general store and watch the *Mickey Mouse Club* program.

As a young child, Sue remembers when the drug store had a fountain and she would sit on the barstool and spoon into a marshmallow sundae.

Sue became a McNary High School cheerleader and she remembers the fierce competition between McNary, where Pinetop teens attended school, and Lakeside. It was while in high school she met Sonny Penrod, who lived in Pinetop. Sonny's father was Reuben "Buster" Penrod, whose father was Ephraim Penrod, a son of patriarch William L. Penrod.

She said that the people of McNary and Pinetop were very close and they almost considered the two towns an extension of each other.

After high school graduation, Sue moved to Phoenix for a short time and attended a business college. Sonny would commute on weekends to see her.

Sue said she wasn't all that thrilled driving in Phoenix traffic and, besides, she missed the pine trees in the White Mountains. Sonny and Sue married shortly thereafter, in 1960, and she has lived in Pinetop ever since.

Her father-in-law operated a grocery store in Pinetop and he told Sue that the town's first settler, Johnny Phipps, was buried in an unmarked grave in the meadow. An apple tree was at the head of the grave and another apple tree at the foot, Sue Penrod said she was told.

She was shown where Phipps was believed to be buried. There was nothing there to distinguish a gravesite. She and her Girl Scout troops outlined the area between the two trees with rocks, then held a fundraising project and raised about $50 to build a fence around the site.

Sue said she was also told that three other persons were buried in the meadow but their whereabouts today are unknown. A grave marker was there at one time, but it long ago disappeared.

Sue and Edith Wilson are on the Pinetop Cemetery board. It is their job to maintain the cemetery. There are 628 people buried in the cemetery and it is full. Only a space or two remain for a loved-one to be buried next to a spouse. When Sue took over the job on the cemetery board, some of the wooden markers had been knocked down. Who is buried in some of the gravesites is unknown.

And there is controversy on the origin of the cemetery site. The Penrod family say William L. Penrod donated the land, but the Adair family said that John Adair, who married William Penrod's granddaughter, donated the land. It is not known for certain who owned the land. Through the years, the cemetery came under county control and it was then passed on to the cemetery board to maintain it.

At the entrance of the cemetery, a person can look toward the west and see the sparkling water of Fred's Lake. Fred Smith and Fred Evans damned up a spring and built the lake, Sue said.

People paid for the fish they caught there by the pound. A restaurant on the edge of the lake served dinners for many years. The entire operation closed down for a few years and more recently a buyer has made the place into a bed-and-breakfast retreat.

A dump used to be in the trees beyond the lake, Sue said. Another dump was a couple miles away, where Pine Lake is now located. Some treasures could be found in the dump.

"That's where I got my first ironing board," said Sue, laughing.

Sue Penrod

Evacuation

Pinetop-Lakeside became a ghost town for a week in June of 2002, when residents had to evacuate in fear that the raging Rodeo-Chediski wildfire would sweep into town, devouring houses and businesses like a fire-breathing dragon attacking an anthill.

National Guardsmen, sheriff posse members and Pinetop-Lakeside police patrolled the deserted streets and neighborhoods. Firefighters stood by, waiting for the onslaught. Fortunately, for us, the fire was contained just outside Show Low and we were allowed to return home.

People west of Show Low weren't as fortunate. The fire consumed homes and businesses and hundreds of people were left homeless.

• • •

The day the Rodeo fire broke out near Cibecue, and a huge billow of smoke loomed skyward for Pinetop residents to see, the radio broadcast reported the fire appeared to be no threat to homes and no extra help from local firefighters or the forest service was needed.

Nevertheless, the next day, Pinetop-Lakeside Police Chief Terry Ringey and Police Commander Randy Harris drove to Cibecue to look over the fire and talk to Apache tribal police.

However, the fire jumped the creek bed (where Apache and Bureau of Indian Affairs firefighters had thought it would be contained) and all fiery hell broke loose.

Harris said the fire roared from 1,200 acres to 50,000 acres in just one day. Ringey and Harris drove to Whiteriver to confer with others and they decided they had better head back to town and start making evacuation plans.

Harris said they turned part of the police building into an emergency center and began pouring over maps of the town's incorporated limits, charting evacuation procedures.

But as the fire continued to consume hundreds of acres in one gulp, Navajo County Sheriff Gary Butler called and asked if the Pinetop-Lakeside Police Department would handle evacuation plans for the unincorporated areas from Wagon Wheel through Pinetop Country Club that borders the Fort Apache Indian Reservation.

"We grid the whole area," Harris said.

At one point, the police department received an emergency call that the fire would sweep into Pinetop-Lakeside in eight hours. All the police personnel were called into headquarters at 1 a.m. to begin the evacuation, but then a call came saying that the fire wouldn't be there in eight hours.

"For (the next) 48 hours it was on and off.. up and down," Harris said.

In the meantime, he sent officers into the community as a "courtesy notification," telling residents that if they were uncomfortable because of the advancing fire they might want to consider leaving town. This was not a mandatory evacuation order, just a courtesy call, he said.

Police and firefighters in town waited. The fire had started on Tuesday, June 18, and by nightfall on Saturday, June 22, the evacuation order was made for all residents of Pinetop-Lakeside, Hon-Dah and McNary. Show Low got the call hours earlier. (Communities west of Show Low were evacuated earlier in the week.) It was feared, because of the fire's erratic behavior, it would jump U.S. 60 south of Show Low for a clear run to Pinetop-Lakeside.

Harris said that since many residents heeded the "courtesy" suggestion and left earlier in the week, it made the evacuation much easier. Fewer cars were on the road at the same time.

Harris estimated about 20,000 persons in the area east of Wagon Wheel were evacuated. Maricopa County sent sheriff posse members and the Arizona National Guard sent troops to help out the Pinetop-Lakeside police. They set up road blocks and patrolled the entire area.

All but a couple of the police department's 25-person staff stayed behind while they sent their spouses and children out of town. However, Harris said, about 100 residents refused to evacuate and they were ordered not to leave their own properties.

A few hundred Type I firefighters set up camp at Blue Ridge High School. Colorful pup tents blossomed across the athletic field.

Utility personnel and some service and retail people stayed behind. Johnny Angel's and Lotus Garden provided food for these essential people.

Harris said he contacted Lakeside Cinema and movies were shown free of charge (snacks available for sale) for police, firefighters and guardsmen.

Meanwhile, Harris was concerned that should the fire sweep into town, the police building might burn. He locked vital records inside a fireproof safe and moved 10 heavy filing cabinets into the jail cell made of concrete block.

The Forest Service also expressed concern and placed water hoses on the town hall building.

Each day that went by the police breathed a little easier, and at 8 a.m. Saturday, June 29, Pinetop-Lakeside lifted the evacuation order and the roadblocks were dismantled.

Mayor Ginny Handorf sat in the bed of her pickup truck with a sign at the town's eastern edge and welcomed home the returning residents. Some even waved and honked the car horn at her.

Harris said that during the whole ordeal there was no looting, no accidents, no gridlock, nor any unfortunate incidents. There was one benefit during the evacuation, he said. The police learned about some drug activity in town and they were able to arrest people and haul them to jail in Holbrook. Those who were with them and not charged were taken out of town, and the police told the National Guardsmen at the roadblock not to let these people back in.

"They said 'you don't have to worry because we're not coming back,'" Harris said. "We got rid of this criminal element."

The final tally of the Rodeo-Chediski Fire that swept through communities west of Show Low was 468,130 acres consumed, nearly one billion Ponderosa, juniper and oak trees burned, and more than 420 structures, mostly homes, destroyed.

• • •

Jim Paxon became the voice describing the destructive force of "The Monster" fire with flames roaring as high as 400 feet and speeding toward White Mountain communities.

Paxon, spokesman for the firefighting effort, explained in down-to-earth terms what was going on: where the battle lines were being drawn; what happens when the fire crowns; why the wildfire created a massive plume;

Jim Paxon

what happens when the plume bursts and creates its own weather pattern, and, what is slurry made of?

Paxon had a calming effect on the thousands of mountain residents who tuned to daily 11 a.m. news conferences. Residents wondered if their homes might become a smoldering black mass of twisted rubble.

He didn't mince words or sugar-coated anything. Some of the things he said we didn't like, although we wanted the truth, no matter how much it hurt. "Fire is neither good nor bad," he said. "Fire is natural. And if you live in a forested environment fire will visit you."

He always gave us a thread of hope, though, assuring us the firefighters had a plan and they were on the attack. We clung to this hope, even as Pinetop residents were evacuated on the fifth day of the fire, and the score was Mother Nature 5 and Man 0.

Then a few days later, while we were sitting in our adoptive homes, whether at American Red Cross shelters, relatives' homes or in motel rooms, Paxon came before us on television and said:

"We have to emphasize that Mother Nature is still in control, but we're on the scoreboard. We haven't been there for eight days. We're making progress."

For the first time we smiled.

Mother Nature 8 and Man 1.

Paxon became an instant folk hero in the White Mountains. We could put our total trust in him, although he was a U.S. government employee. Women literally fell in love with him, though he was a married man. One divorced mother of two in her early 20s readily admitted she had a "crush" on him. A grandmother-aged woman said she adored him and wished he were single. When we were allowed to return home, a large sign at a Show Low restaurant announced: "We Love Jim Paxon." If Paxon would have announced he was running for public office in the White Mountains, he would have been voted in on the spot.

Paxon's fame was not only in the White Mountains. He became an international media figure. His reports on the Rodeo-Chediski fire were carried on CNN, and he was quoted on radio stations across Europe, through the BBC. The *New York Times* interviewed him. And he was honored by being allowed to throw out the first pitch at an Arizona Diamondbacks baseball game in Phoenix.

When not on the fire line somewhere in the United States, Paxon was the district ranger for the Gila National Forest in Truth or Consequences, N.M. He also farms there and raises hay. For more than 20 years he was a firefighter digging fire lines. He quit and became a Forest Service ranger and information officer because his body was taking longer to recover after each fire, he said.

Several weeks after evacuees came home, Show Low city councilman Rick Fernau flew Paxon and his wife, Debbie, from their New Mexico home back to the White Mountains. Paxon was the special guest at Firefighter Friday, an event held at Silver Creek Golf Course to honor those who fought the Rodeo-Chediski fire.

"What a resilient community," Paxon told us. "Do you remember me saying truly the members of the White Mountains are indomitable in spirit. God bless you all.

"...I need you to know that the reason fire was kept out of Show Low was because of the work the White Mountain Apaches had done before the fire...those are the folks who kept fire out of Show Low, Pinetop and Lakeside.

"Man, you all have adopted us; you just met Debbie today and she feels like this is home."

In October, 2002, Paxon rode atop a fire truck as grand marshal of the Pinetop-Lakeside Fall Festival parade. On Jan. 3, 2003, after 33 years with the U.S. Forest Service, Paxon retired. Speaking to a group in Phoenix, as reported in *The Arizona Republic*, he called the Rodeo-Chediski fire "the biggest, fastest, most aggressive, most climatic, awesome fire I've ever seen."

Ready to move when fire strikes

Businesses display signs thanking firefighters after Rodeo-Chediski Fire evacuation

THANK YOU FOR
SAVING
OUR COMMUNITY

THANK YOU
PINETOP FIRE DEPT.
Hoffman
BROKER

• • •

All was not right after the 30,000 evacuees came back to their homes. Blame reportedly became rampant. A lady from Heber told her co-workers in Show Low that many people in the Heber-Overgaard area were angry at the U.S. Forest Service. More firefighters and equipment were used to save Show Low, Pinetop and Lakeside from burning than were sent to fight the fire that destroyed dozens of homes in Overgaard.

Leonard Gregg, an Apache and part-time firefighter, was arrested for starting the Rodeo fire. He said he needed work to pay bills. A federal judge in March 2004 sentenced the arsonist to 10 years in prison and ordered him to pay nearly $28 million in restitution at $100 per month. That means it would take Gregg 23,235 years to get completely out of debt. Valinda Jo Elliott, who started the Chediski blaze with a signal fire after she became lost on the Indian reservation, was not criminally charged. The Rodeo and Chediski fires merged to create Arizona's largest and most devastating wildfire.

Stories were told on the reservation that some business owners in the White Mountains refused service to Indians. Some of the Apaches reportedly were afraid to venture off the reservation to buy supplies.

As the bad feeling against the Apaches grew, a group of Protestant pastors in Pinetop, Show Low and Lakeside organized a prayer and praise service for their members to meet with their White Mountain Apache brethren.

(It was learned days after the event that this apparent strife was just a rumor that mushroomed, but, at the time, seemed very true.)

On Saturday, July 27, 2002, about 60 congregants from several White Mountain churches drove about 25 miles into the heart of the reservation for the 6 p.m. service at the Assemblies of God Church at Canyon Day, a few miles south of Whiteriver, the tribe's capital. About 15 Indians attended the service.

"There is a lot of blaming going on...no Indians allowed," said the white pastor of the Canyon Day church. "I wonder how much God was in it. If it wasn't for this tragedy, we wouldn't be here today."

A Lakeside pastor recalled that 426 structures were burned by the Rodeo-Chediski fire including more than 250 homes. No one was seriously hurt and there was not one fatality. Pinetop, Lakeside and Show Low were spared.

"The Forest Service would like you to believe it was Mother Nature. It was Father God. God really did protect us from this monster fire."

The pastor asked in his prayer for God to comfort those who lost their homes. And for those who were spared from the flames, "we thank You for Your goodness to us."

Another White Mountain pastor said he hoped this service of unity between white men and Indians would spread across the White Mountains.

"We are eager to keep harmony of oneness," he said. "Forgive us for segregating ourselves of color...we are one blood. We call an end of division and segregation in the congregations."

A Lakeside Baptist minister announced that his church is serious about ending any semblance of segregation between white and Indian churches. The Lakeside church had recently become a "sister" church with a non-Baptist congregation in the Apache town of Cibecue, near where the Rodeo fire started.

Throughout the two-hour service, the 75 white and Indian Christian believers spent a lot of time in prayers. Circles of four and five people formed across the auditorium. White men and Indians held hands and fervently repented for being judgmental, asking that this love and unity shown that night between two races would take hold "across this Mountain."

• • •

The 2002 evacuation was a wake-up call for us. No longer can we live in the forest under canopies of pine boughs and watch the little animals such as blue jays, squirrels and chipmunks joyfully play around us without concern.

We can't let Mother Nature take her natural course to correct our failings. We learned that man has mismanaged the forests for 150 years, and we were just as guilty by mismanaging our *own* properties.

Pinetop-Lakeside town council was the first town on the Mountain to pass, in 2003, a fire-wise ordinance, requiring homeowners to clean up their properties and eliminate greenery and dead wooden fuels too close to homes.

And we must nourish our trees. Jim Paxon, who is regarded as a White Mountain hero for his efforts to educate us about wildfires, spoke to a few dozen of us at a Pinetop Garden Club meeting in the Fall of 2003.

The forests have not been thinned and the underbrush not removed, he said. In 1850, about 30 to 40 pines stood in clumps on each acre with lots of open space. Today, it is not unusual to have 600 or more trees per acre. One culprit is the Endangered Species Act that prevented much of the necessary thinning of trees.

"We created something Mother Nature can't cope with," Paxon said. "The Forest you see is not what the Good Lord put there. We either do it (manage the forests) or Mother Nature will do it for us (with wildfires)."

When man first moved into the forest more than 100 years ago, cattle and sheep, along with deer, antelope and elk browsed, keeping the undergrowth in check. The sheepmen and cattlemen have since moved out and masses of homes moved in, pushing the browsing animals deeper into the woods. Lumbermen cut mature trees and small pines mushroomed, creating a jungle-like forest.

Thinning efforts have been thwarted by environmentalists.

The drought has made the forest more vulnerable to wildfires. Trees so close to each other become sick, easy targets for the dreaded pine-bark beetles. The beetles, we learned, won't attack healthy trees.

A large Ponderosa pine killed by bark beetles may cost as much as $200 to cut down and haul away. Tree climbers (not to be confused with the tree-huggers who helped the forests to get in this mess) are hired to cut off dead limbs high in the crowns of trees. Juniper and other bushes near our houses must be removed, so they won't create a ladder effect for a fire to reach our homes.

Paxon said a 10-inch diameter tree needs to drink as much as 20 gallons of water a day between Easter and Thanksgiving. An alligator Juniper the same size drinks more per day, up to 50 gallons.

The trees are competing for water. There are from 60- to 70-foot tap roots on 100-foot trees. Feeder roots go as far out as the drip line of the tree's crown.

Our water bills are higher now, because we are learning to deepwater our pine trees, a task that we once relied on Mother Nature to do.

Paxon quoted an expert, saying that the drought will continue for years to come.

"We are in the fifth year (2003) of a 15 to 20-year drought," Paxon said. "If you love your trees, cut them."

Paxon practiced what he preached. He thinned the forest with prescribed burns. "I burned 114,000 acres of forest on my district in the 14 years as a (U.S. Forest) district ranger...some of my peers think I'm a pyromaniac. I never let a fire get away."

Ron Kemble, a certified arborist in the White Mountains, suggests that homeowners living in the forest broadcast fertilizer (6-20-20) over all of the property in June or October/November, and the trees should be watered deep every 20 to 30 days, especially between rains.

Kemble then drops a bombshell.

"Do you know there were no Ponderosa pines here 800 years ago. They were at 9,000 feet or above."

Climatic changes moved these trees to lower elevations and now climatic changes are moving these trees back to higher elevations.

That's why the Ponderosa pines are dying in record numbers, because of the drought and bark beetles around Prescott, which is just a little above 5,000 feet in elevation. Other hard-hit areas are trees around Crown King, Horsethief Basin, Pine, Strawberry, and bands of trees near Flagstaff and Winslow.

And Pinetop, at 7,200 feet elevation, is not that much behind.

A welcome sight. Dark clouds over the White Mountains.

Old ranch buildings in Alpine

Winter arrives in Pinetop

Jeannette Luptak dishes up dinner at Big Lake campground. Circa: 1970's

Martin Luptak fishes on a cold day
at Big Lake. Circa: 1970's

My wife and my parents enjoy the warmth
of a campfire at Big Lake. Circa: 1970's

A leisure stroll into the woods

The meadow across from Hannagan Meadow

Sweep Across the Mountain

"Are you going to the races?" a waitress at Bear Wallow Cafe in Alpine asked a co-worker.

A visitor at the counter mused: *Races? Is there a horse or dog track here in the boonies?*

No, worm races behind the town's Ye Olde Tavern, he learned.

"Is this the biggest event here each year?" the visitor asked Old Timer sitting a couple of stools away.

"Yep."

"Whose idea to have a worm race?"

"When you have one restaurant and one tavern in town you have lots of time to think these things up. After the race we go fishing. Here's your reward, we tell the worm."

The worm event is held annually on the Saturday closest to July Fourth. It begins with a morning parade. The two race tracks consist of 4-x-4 sheets of plywood, heavily varnished and slick, with four-inch circles painted in the middle. Two worms race at a time, with their progress measured after two minutes. Worm-owners squirt water on their worms to encourage them to move faster.

At one recent race, spectators and worm-racers crowded under two tents behind the bar. Some worms rebelled and didn't move. Others just crawled an inch or two. Once in a while a worm went crazy and crawled off the table. The owner hurriedly picked it up plopping it in the circle and let it wiggle some more. One worm slithered and slid 62 inches in just two minutes.

One man had an idea to stimulate his worm: "I'll put Tabasco sauce in the water." Another man, after watching the worm crawl off the table, said the worm must have been on steroids.

Worms, all nightcrawlers, are sold for $5 each, with proceeds used to buy books for Alpine Elementary School library. The top three winners in each of two heats of this "bookworm" event received trophies.

One recent Worm Day Parade on Alpine's main street consisted of about a dozen entries—six teenage girls riding horses, a man driving a John Deere tractor, Alpine's two fire department vehicles (Rescue #1 and Engine #1), 12 motorcyclists wearing black, a pickup with a sign "Remembering fallen firefighters," and someone dressed in a jelly bean costume throwing small packets of jelly beans to the 100 to 150 spectators.

If you miss any of the parade, just hang around a few minutes. The entire group will turn around and go back down the same parade route to disperse where they started.

Living in or visiting the White Mountains is just plain lots of fun. Activities, some off-the-wall such as the worm race, include small-town parades where participants throw candy to spectators, car shows, golf and softball tournaments, dog-sled races and kids' fishing derbies. Another big plus is the cooler temperatures up here in the summer, much lower than in the Phoenix and Tucson metropolitan areas.

For visitor and resident alike, there is fishing in dozens of sparkling lakes, camping, hunting, golfing, horseback riding, water-skiing, hiking on hundreds of miles of marked trails, biking, rock-hounding and just relaxing in the shade of a large pine tree. Do you want to rent a lake? You can in the White Mountains. And, in the winter, there is down-hill and cross-country skiing, snowboarding, snowmobiling, sleigh rides and ice fishing. Ice skating, too, if the winter is cold enough. The area abounds with fine restaurants, motels, RV camps and resorts, including Hon-Dah Casino, which also provides live entertainment. People drive up here to see the fall colors. And, at night, you can see the stars shining in the sky.

All this within minutes, or less than couple of hours, from Pinetop. Although not everyone will agree, the White Mountains begin at Show Low and stretch east into New Mexico. In addition to Pinetop and surrounding communities, the White Mountains include the Fort Apache Indian Reservation, Greer, Springerville-Eagar and South to Alpine and Hannagan Meadow lodge and a few miles beyond. The forest stops before it gets to St. Johns, Taylor, Snowflake and Holbrook and these towns are technically not part of the White Mountains. However, these communities have played an integral part in the development of White Mountain settlements. Most of the White Mountains are in Navajo and Apache counties, and Holbrook and St. Johns are the county seats, respectively.

St. Johns—Mexicans from New Mexico, descendents of the Spanish Conquistadors, arrived first and settled in St. Johns (the town was first called San Juan) in 1872. The first ones were Jose Seavedra and his father, who arrived in a two-wheel ox cart. They built a bridge over the Little Colorado River so their sheep could cross over. The road from Zuni to Fort Apache had to cross the river there and the Seavedras made money allowing freighters to use the bridge. Then came the Mormons, and, later, the Texas cattlemen. Since the Mexicans were mainly sheepherders, conflicts arose between the sheepmen and cattlemen. There were shootings and killings.

Springerville—Juan Baca arrived in 1862, and later brought his family. The first Anglos were Marion Clark, who was the first settler of Show Low, and William Milligan, Anthony Long and Joe McCollough. Milligan in his first year raised 800,000 pounds of barley, which he sold to Fort Apache. In 1876, he built a sawmill. This area became a mecca for the outlaw and horse thief. In the 1870s, Henry Springer moved in from Albuquerque and opened a store. He gave credit to the outlaws for feed, seed and supplies, and within a year he went broke and left town.

Holbrook—The Atlantic & Pacific Railroad (later called Santa Fe) put Holbrook on the map, when the train came to northern Arizona. Through the years, a few settlements had been established around the area. Some were Mormon settlements, and Kit Carson started one in 1863 to serve the Army in its campaign against the Navajo Indians.

For a time, supplies brought in by train were unloaded onto horse-drawn wagons and the freighters hauled them to such places as Fort Apache.

It seemed Holbrook vied with Tombstone for the title of the toughest town in the west. It is reported that 26 men were shot to death in just one year in Holbrook. Northern Arizona became a hideout for outlaws. Many were driven out of Texas and New Mexico when the law there became prevalent. This part of Arizona was still wide open territory for criminals.

Holbrook boasted of not even having a church until 1912, the only county seat in the United States without one. The Bucket of Blood Saloon was the favorite place in town to gather.

Fights between sheepmen and cattlemen brewed. This was augmented in the mid-1880s when the Hashknife outfit from Texas received a million acres from the railroad's holdings and it shipped from 30,000 to 40,000 cattle to northern Arizona to roam at will on open range, both on and off their land. Cattle from local ranches got mixed up with the Hashknife's. Branding irons sizzled calves' hides and it didn't matter whose calves they belonged to—the Hashknife's or local ranchers.

Some of these Hashknife cowpokes were reportedly wanted for various crimes both within and outside the state.

James Jennings in his book, *The Freight Rolled,* said that once the young people of Taylor gathered for a dance in the schoolhouse.

Some Hashknife men with guns drawn walked in and ordered the "ladies on the right; gents on the left." The gunmen told the young women to undress, which they reluctantly started to do. Meanwhile, a young man at the dance slipped unnoticed out a rear door and he grabbed from a wood pile a piece of wood resembling a gun. He hurried to the front door behind the cowboys and yelled for them to drop their weapons. They complied, and the young men of Taylor picked up the guns. Dick Shumway, the wooden-gun holder, ordered the cowboys to leave "and don't come back!" The cowboys left.

Eventually, the law arrived in northern Arizona, and the outlaw breed was tamed. One lawman was Commodore Perry Owens. He went after the Clanton gang which had moved into the Springerville area from Tombstone. Owens later became the first sheriff of Navajo County.

Show Low—The early beginnings of Show Low, citing settlers such as Corydon E. Cooley, Marion Clark and Henry Huning, are told in previous chapters. In 1903, Huning sold all his holdings to six Mormon Colonizers for $13,500. One of these Mormons was Niels Hansen, who later help colonize Lakeside.

Show Low's population in 1910 reached 201 residents. It increased to 258 in 1920, and swelling to nearly 8,300 in 2002. Show Low has become the largest town in the White Mountains and provides the major shopping and services in the area. Wal-Mart, K-Mart and Home Depot are its major merchants. There are several car dealers scattered within the city limits.

Fort Apache Indian Reservation—On Nov. 9, 1871, President Ulysses S. Grant signed an executive order establishing the 1.7-million acre Fort Apache Indian Reservation.

In the 1950s, the White Mountain Apache Tribe began to develop the reservation as a recreation haven for both Indian and whiteman alike. There was resistance. The Salt River Project wanted all the water running off the reservation that drained into the Salt and Verde rivers to flow into SRP's reservoirs northwest of Phoenix. The tribe resisted, and lawsuits were filed and defeated. The tribe built 26 lakes for recreational purposes. There also are more than 420 miles of streams—some stocked with fish—and over 1,000 camping sites. Some of the lakes have stores, boat rental facilities and cabins to rent.

Sunrise Ski Resort consists of three mountains and 65 ski runs. Hon-Dah Resort & Casino features a luxury hotel with 128 oversized rooms and the largest conference/convention center in northeastern Arizona. The casino offers hundreds of slot machines, blackjack tables, a poker room, children's arcade, restaurant, lounge and live entertainment. Across the street from Hon-Dah Casino is an RV park with 198 sites in the pines.

Two fish hatcheries on the reservation are open to the public. Wildlife include elk, bear, mountain lion, deer, antelope and water fowl. Hunting permits are needed for bull elk and other animals. Want to throw a big bash to impress your friends? Rent a lake! The 37-acre Cyclone Lake rents for $400 daily and the 19-acre Hurricane Lake goes for $300 daily.

The Army established Fort Apache at the confluence of the north and east forks of the White River on May 16, 1870 in order to assist the White Mountain Apache people to peacefully protect their lands. For 52 years, there were turbulent periods of conflict, but also times of progressive cooperation between the U.S. government and Indians. The military fort closed in 1922 and a boarding school opened in its place. Today, the 288-acre historic park houses a cultural center and museum. Visitors may take a self-guided walking tour of the fort grounds, including more than 25 buildings. A few miles away are the ancient Kinishba Pueblo ruins.

Greer—Mormons settled in this picturesque valley in 1879. Jacob Noah Butler came here in the 1890s with his two wives, Sarah and Sena and 19 children. He built a cabin with a large common room, kitchen and two bedrooms — one for each family. Molly Crosby married John T. Butler, son of Jacob. She became postmistress in 1903. They built a lodge that could sleep 22 people. At first, people who came to hunt, fish or vacation stayed in it for free, only pitching in to do chores. The lodge, along with others, are favorite places for vacationers today. This hamlet, at 8,500-foot elevation, is also a popular pristine spot for fishing, camping, hiking and relaxing. Beavers splash in the Little Colorado River, which runs through the Valley. Nearby are Tunnel and Bunch lakes and River Reservoir, favorites for fishermen.

Alpine—In 1876, Anderson Bush built a log home that later became known as Bush Valley Fort to protect early settlers against hostile Indians, including Apache warrior Geronimo. Bush later sold the valley to Mormon homesteaders, who developed the town. At 8,000 feet elevation, summer homes dot the forest. The town is a haven for fishermen, hunters, campers and sightseers. A popular gathering place is the Bear Wallow Cafe. People drive here mainly to shop in the candy and fudge store, and the town annually sponsors a regional chili cook-off.

Snowflake—James Stinson settled here first on Silver Creek. He sold his ranch for 500 head of cattle to Mormons, who settled the area. Before this, Stinson tried to trade his land to James Pearce, who settled south of him.

Pearce declined and instead decided to homestead land. That settlement later became known as Taylor.

Snowflake incorporated in 1919, and immediately town fathers outlawed tobacco sales. Three years later, the town condemned mixed swimming at Silver Creek Dam. A new ordinance allowed males to swim on Tuesdays, Thursdays and Saturdays, and females on Mondays, Wednesdays and Fridays. No one swam on Sundays. The twin-towns of Snowflake/Taylor have more than 100 historical buildings, with 45 sites on the National Historic Registry. Six are open to the public for tours. Mormons in 2002 dedicated a temple in Snowflake, their second in Arizona. Taylor is known throughout the state for its annual sweet corn festival over Labor Day.

Lyman Lake State Park—This lake north of Springerville has no size restriction on boats, allowing for speedboats and water skiing, unlike other lakes in the White Mountains. However, part of the lake is reserved for swimming and fishing. There are hookups and campsites available. A small herd of buffalo owned by the St. Johns Chamber of Commerce reside at the entrance to the park.

Camping—There are 36 campgrounds available in the Apache-Sitgreaves National Forests. Amenities in some of them include stores, drinking water, flush toilets, hot showers and "trailer sanitary stations." The largest campground, with more than 200 campsites, is at Big Lake. There are more than 40 lakes within 40 miles of Pinetop, including Woodlake Lake Park in the heart of Pinetop-Lakeside.

One former Phoenix resident expressed in one word what living year-around in the White Mountains means to him, and the advice he gives visitors:

"Enjoy!"

• • •

How White Mountain communities got their names:

Alpine—Named because of it's alpine altitude (8,000 feet) and also because of Mormons from Alpine, Utah, who bought land in the area. Post Office established Jan. 7, 1885.

Eagar—Named after three Eagar brothers, John, Joel and William. Post Office established Feb. 4, 1898.

Fort Apache—Named in respect for the Apache. Previously the fort was called Camp Ord, Camp Mogollon, Camp Thomas and Camp Apache. Post Office established Aug. 13, 1879.

Greer—On March 12, 1898, when a post office was established, the name was changed from Lee Valley to Greer in honor of a respected citizen, Americus Vispucius Greer. The post office claimed that "Lee Valley" was too long a name.

Holbrook—Formerly known as Horsehead Crossing. Named in 1880 for H.R. Holbrook, first chief engineer of the Atlantic and Pacific Railroad. Post Office established Sept. 18, 1882.

Lakeside—Named for being near Rainbow Lake. Post Office established Oct. 5, 1906.

McNary—Named for lumberman James G. McNary. Post Office established April 8, 1925. Previously, the town's name was Cooley, with a post office under that name established Jan. 17, 1919.

Nutrioso—First settlers killed a beaver (*nutria* in Spanish) and a bear (*oso*). Post Office established April 12, 1883.

Pinetop—Troops from Fort Apache had to ride up the mountain to the saloon for drinks. They would say, let's go to the "Top of the Pines." Another story is a bartender at this saloon had a fuzzy lock of hair that resembled a treetop and the troops called him "pinetop." Post Office established Dec. 9, 1891.

St. John's—Mexican settlers named it to honor St. John's (*San Juan's*) Day, June 24. Post Office established April 5, 1880.

Show Low—This settlement was just too small for its first two residents, Corydon E. Cooley and Marion Clark. Legend says they played a card game and toward the end Cooley needed just one point to win. Clark turned his cards over and said, "If you can show low you win." Cooley threw down his hand of cards and said, "Show Low it is." Post Office established Aug. 19, 1880.

Snowflake—Not named for snowfall, but for the last names of the town's first pioneers—Erastus Snow and William Flake. Post Office established June 27, 1881.

Springerville—Henry Springer, a pioneer merchant, came to this settlement, which was referred to as Omer Ward of the Mormon church. Named after Springer. Post Office established Oct. 29, 1879.

Taylor—Named for John Taylor, third president of the Mormon church. Post Office established March 28, 1881.

Whiteriver—Named after nearby White River. Post Office established Nov. 19, 1896.

Bibliography

The Apaches: Eagles of the Southwest, Donald E. Worcester, University of Oklahoma Press, 1979.
Apaches & Longhorns, Will Croft Barnes, The University of Arizona Press, Tucson, AZ.
Arizona's Amazing Towns: From Wild West to High Tech, Richard Dillon, Four Peaks Press, Tempe, AZ 1992.
Arizona Territory: Post Offices & Postmasters, John and Lillian Theobald, Arizona Historical Foundation, Phoenix, AZ 1961.
Arizona Was The West, James R. Jennings, The Naylor Company, San Antonio, TX, 1970.
Cooley: Army Scout, Arizona Pioneer, Wayside Host, Apache Friend, H.B. Wharfield, self-published, 1966.
Firm as the Mountain: A History of the Show Low, Arizona Stake, 1993.
The Freight Rolled, James R. Jennings, The Naylor Company, San Antonio, TX, 1969.
Hashknife Cowboy: Recollections of Mack Hughes, Stella Hughes, The University of Arizona Press, Tucson, AZ, 1934.
Hidden Highways Arizona, Richard Harris, Ulysses Press, Berkeley, CA, 2001.
Historic Resource Survey of Show Low, Arizona, Pat H. Stein, SWCA Inc., Flagstaff, AZ, 1994.
The Lakeside Years: 1925-1928, Lorenzo Kenneth Lisonbee, self-published journal, 1988.
A Land of Sunshine: Flagstaff and its Surroundings, George H. Tinker, The Arthur H. Clark Company, Glendale, CA, 1969.
The Law of the Gun, Marshall Trimble, Arizona Highways, 1997.
Leora's Quest: Lakeside and Beyond, Leora Peterson Schuck, Peterson Printers, Show Low, AZ, 1980.

Little Colorado Adjudication: Silver Creek Objections: Expert Witness Report, Shelly C. Dudley, Salt River Project, Feb. 1994.
Memories of Lakeside School: 1906-1963, a volunteer effort for the Lakeside School reunion, July 2000.
Men Who Matched The Mountains: The Forest Service in the Southwest, Edwin A. Tucker and George Fitzpatrick, United States Department of Agriculture, 1972.
Mixed-Bloods, Apaches and Cattle Barons: Documents for a History of the Livestock Economy on the White Mountain Reservation, Arizona, Thomas R. McGuire, Arizona State Museum, University of Arizona, Tucson, AZ, 1980.
No Place for Angels, Roscoe G. Willson, The Arizona Republic, Phoenix, AZ; Arizona Silhouettes, Tucson, AZ, 1958.
On the Border with Crook, John G. Bourke, University of Nebraska Press, Lincoln, NE and London, 1971 (first published in 1891).
On the Road to Nowhere: A History of Greer, Arizona 1879-1979, Karen Miller Applewhite, self-published journal, 1979.
"Pinetop/Lakeside 1885-1985," Jo Baeza, White Mountains of Arizona, Vol. 31, 1985.
Ranch Wife, Jo Jeffers, The University of Arizona Press, Tucson, AZ and London, 1964.
Rural Electrification in Multiethnic Arizona: A Study of Power, Urbanization and Change, a dissertation for the degree doctor of philosophy by Leah S. Glaser, Arizona State University, May 2002.
A Tribute to the Lakeside Pioneers, a collection by various authors edited and published by Karen La Duke, 1987.
Vanished Arizona, Martha Summerhayes, University of Nebraska Press, Lincoln, NE, 1979; reprint of second edition (1911) published by Salem Press, Salem, Mass. (Martha Summerhayes, 1864-1911).

Author's Notes and Acknowledgments

In my over 30 years of traveling to the White Mountains to fish and camp, I drove through Pinetop many times, but I don't have any recollection of what it looked like I don't think I ever stopped to eat or even buy gasoline in the town. Pinetop was just as familiar to me as Timbuktu.

Then, when I moved here and had a chance to look around, I walked into the local bookstore and asked if they had a book on Pinetop's history. There wasn't, and the owner said she wished someone would write one.

I shunned the advice I learned from attending numerous writing conferences, where the speakers urged writers, especially those writing their first book, to write about something they knew about. As far as I was concerned, when I accepted the challenge to write Pinetop's history, a penrod was some kind of a new writing instrument. I foolishly thought writing a history on Pinetop and its White Mountain neighbors would be a snap. It wasn't. Early on I discovered mistakes and contradictions in published material I found in libraries and other places. Even gravestones had wrong information. Delbert and Albert Penrod were twins, both born, obviously, in 1864. However, on Albert's tombstone he was "born" in 1868, while his twin brother's grave marker listed the correct year of 1864. Even people I interviewed gave wrong information.

Consider:

*Johnny Phipps, Pinetop's first settler, died in 1890 according to *Arizona's Names X Marks the Place*. **Fact:** Johnny Phipps was still alive in 1895, when a court ruled he and others were entitled to certain waters for irrigation purposes.

*Pinetop Post Office was established Jan. 31, 1895 with Edward E. Bradshaw as postmaster, according to *Arizona's Names X Marks the Place*. Pinetop Post Office was established Dec. 9, 1891 with Bradshaw as postmaster, according to *Arizona Territory Post Offices & Postmasters*.

*William Penrod moved to Pinetop in the fall of 1886, according to Mrs. Ralph Penrod in *White Mountains of Arizona,* Fall 1970. William Penrod moved to Pinetop in 1887, according to Leora Peterson Schuck in *A Tribute to the Lakeside Pioneers.*

*A writer said in a magazine article that until 1885 the town of Pinetop was called "Penrod." The Penrods didn't settle there until 1886 or 1887.

Arizona Was The West reported that Harry Springer opened a store in 1875, the beginning of Springerville. The regional Chamber of Commerce said the town was founded in 1879 around the trading post operated by *Henry* Springer. Harry or Henry?

Mistakes and contradictions do happen. Some are made by sloppy reporting, but, more often than not, wrong information unintentionally creeps into both verbal interviews and published works. Oldtimers' memories sometime fail on facts that occurred some 50, 60 or 70 years ago. And embellishments are not uncommon. Hand-me-down historical facts sometime get distorted. Ever play the game where one person in a group whispers something into a neighbor's ear, then that person tells someone else and so on until the message goes around the room? What the last person hears and repeats often doesn't even come close to what the first person said.

I apologize if there are mistakes in this book. I tried as much as possible to collaborate facts. Some pioneers mentioned in this book didn't live stellar existences. They had flaws, and I tried to give a true picture of them—both the good and the bad. It shows people's warts along with their cute dimples. If it didn't, I failed to be objective in the way I presented their profiles, the area and historical events.

I was very fortunate to get information on Martin Penrod and Jake Renfro from recorded family histories that, as far as I know, have never been published for the general public. Lu Anne Frost, deputy town clerk with Pinetop-Lakeside, whose husband, Roger, is a grandson of Martin Penrod, let me copy the family history on Martin Penrod's life. And Linda Renfro, librarian at Blue Ridge High School, whose husband, Gary, grandson of Renfro, provided the information on Jake Renfro's life. Both histories were written by other family members years ago.

Thanks also must go to the people I interviewed and the members of the Pinetop-Lakeside Historical Society, who helped me enormously with the gathering of facts, profiles and pictures. Special thanks to Georgia Dysterheft, Marion Hansen, Raymond Johnson and Raymond Lee. I appreciate the friendly help I received from the volunteers at the family room center at the Show Low LDS church. Norman Mead, publisher of *Arizona's White Mountains* for 50 years, was also a great help, and looking at some of the back issues was useful in researching this book.

Mike and Tama White with Ghost River Images in Tucson put this book together. Tama edited it and corrected my silly spelling, grammar and wordy mistakes. Laura L. Haney gave me permission to use on the back cover her dramatic photograph of the Rodeo-Chediski Fire. Thanks Mike, Tama and Laura.

My wife, Dawn, must get the most credit of all. She had to put up with my grumpy mood while I was researching and writing this book. And, she took the picture that was used on the cover. We decided the cover should show Woodland Lake in Pinetop. She went there and clicked a picture, and then waited while I shot a roll of film, taking various angles of the lake and surrounding trees. I even went back a few days later to take more pictures. Finally, we laid all the pictures on the table. Hers was by far the best.

Index

A

Abdul-Jabbar, Kareem 69
Adair, Clements 14, 36
Adair, Dan 94
Adair, Delbert 36
Adair, Delbert, Jr. 34
Adair Drive 115
Adair, Genevieve 36
Adair, John 35, 37, 40, 136
Adair, John Robin 35
Adair, John Washington 33
Adair, Leslie 36
Adair, Lloyd Edwin 36
Adair Spring 82, 84
Adair, Virginia 36
Adams, David 29
Adams, Della 93
Adams, Len 93
Adams, Lon 93
Alchesay 41
Alchesay Drive 115
Alpine 159, 160, 161, 165, 167
American Red Cross 144
Amos, Abraham Lincoln (Abe) 39, 40, 93
Amos, C.D. (Dick) 39, 40, 93
Amos, Len 39, 40
Amos, William 9, 39, 40, 82, 84
antelope 164
Apache County 100, 161
Apache firefighters 140
Apache Kid 77
Apache Lumber Company 89
Apache Railroad 129
Apache Tribe 90, 91
Apache-Sitgreaves National Forest 166
Apaches, ancestors of vii

Apaches, Mimbres 25
Aravaipas Apaches 47
Archaic Culture people vi
Arizona Diamondbacks 145
Arizona Game and Fish Department 101
Arizona Highways 127
Arizona National Guard *141*
Arizona Office of Economic Planning & Development 119
Arizona White Mountains magazine 3
Atlantic & Pacific Railroad 162, 167
Axline, Thelma 126

B

Baca, Juan 162
Baeza, Jo 71, 115, 125
Baeza, Luis Mario 127
Barnes, Will C. 44
BBC 145
bear 130, 131, 164
Bear Wallow Cafe 159
beaver 165
Bernard, Nelson 112
Bickel, Dub and Virginia 68
Big Lake 103, 166
Billy Creek vi, viii, 3, 80, 84, 85, 127
Bittorf 121
Bittorf, Mary Ellen 120
Black River vii, 45, 47
Blue 103, 121, 122, 141
Blue Moon Dance Hall 36
Blue Ridge High School 85, 98
Blue Ridge schools 96
Blue Ridge Unified School District 98
Bowles, Mabel 64, 72, 126
Bradshaw, Edward E. 3, 4, 22
Brown, Bill 127
Brown, J.P.S. 127
Brown, Paula 127
browsing animals 150
Bucket of Blood Saloon 162
Buckskin Pete 25

buffalo 166
Bunch lake 165
Bureau of Indian Affairs 101, 102
Bureau of Indian Affairs firefighters 140
Bush, Anderson 165
Bush Valley Fort 165
Butler, Gary 140
Butler, Hal 17
Butler, Jacob Noah 10, 165
Butler, John T. 165
Butler, Sarah Ann 10

C

C&E Office Supply 122
Cady, M.W. 90
Camp Apache 167
Camp Mogollon 167
Camp Ord 167
Camp Thomas 167
Camp Verde 29
campgrounds 166
Canyon Day 148
Carson, Albert 93
Carson, Kit 162
Carson, Lee 93
Carter, Gary 132
Carter, Joe 132
Casa Malpais vii
cattlemen 161
Channel 3 123
Charlie Clark's Log Cabin Cafe 67
Charlie Clark's Steak House 59, 71
Chavez, Jane 121
chipmunks 131
Chiricahua Apaches 43, 47
Christmas Tree restaurant 85
Cibecue 45, 91, 139, 149
Cibiano 48
Civilian Conservation Corps (CCC) camp 112
Clanton gang 163
Clark, Charlie 58, 59, 60, 67, 110, 126

Clark, Dolly 62
Clark, Marguerite Elizabeth (Buddy) 62, 64
Clark, Marion 29, 77, 162, 163, 168
Clark, Thelma Wetsel 67
Cluff, Alfred 29
Cluff Cienega 89
CNN 145
Cochise 44
College of Education at Arizona State University 96
Colorado River 99
Colvin, John 40
Cooley 90, 115, 167
Cooley, Belle 93
Cooley, Belle Crook 39
Cooley, Charlie 93
Cooley, Cora 28, 93
Cooley, Corydon E. 8, 25, 26, 39, 40, 77, 89, 93, 163, 168
Cooley, Lillie 28, 31, 93
Cooley, Molly 28, 39
Corduroy Creek 31, 40
Crandall, Abner 79
Crook, General George 29, 44, 46
Crosby, Frank 60, 64, 71, 110, 113
Crosby, Molly 165
Crosby Road 113
Crosser, John 74
Crouse, C.W. 40
Crown King 152
Cyclone Lake 164

D

Dana, Joe 36
Daniel, Louis 36
deer 164
Dew Drop Inn 68, 71, 74, 75, 109
Diablo 44, 48, 50
Dragon Inn 68
Dudley, Shelly C. 4
Dunlap, Kevin 117
Dysterheft, Dr. Arnold 90

E

Eagar 167
Eagar brothers, John, Joel and William 167
elk 131, 164
Elliott, Valinda Jo 148
Ellsworth, Frank 30
Endangered Species Act 150
England 130
Eskiole 44
Evans, Fred 136

F

Fairview 79
Fernandez, Bob 113, 115, 126
FHA 16
Finney, Jim 17
First Baptist Church 109
First Interstate Bank 121
Fish, John L. 40, 82
Fish, M.L. 101
Flake, William 82, 168
Ford, Henry 60
Forestdale 30
Fort Apache 2, 5, 19, 29, 30, 31, 33, 40, 43, 44, 45, 47, 52, 64, 79, 89, 91, 99, 101, 110, 140, 161, 162, 164, 167
Fort Apache Indian Reservation 1
Fort Bowie 43
Foster, Lucille 95
Fred's Lake 127, 136
freighters 2
Frizell, George 25

G

Gene Autry 125
George, Sharon 55
Geronimo 43, 44, 165
Gibson, Bill 68, 70
Gibson, Tricia 70
Girl Scout troop 136

Glaser, Leah S. 99
Goar, Buck 120
Goldwater, Barry 134
Grant, Ulysses S. 44, 47, 164
Green, Maj. John 29
Greer 134, 161, 165, 167
Greer, Americus Vispucius 167
Gregg, Leonard 148

H

Hall, George 10, 40
Hall, John 4
Hall Lane 115
Handorf, Ginny 142
Hannagan Meadow 103, 161
Hansen, Hans 4, 79, 93
Hansen, Hans, Jr. 79, 80
Hansen, Horace 94
Hansen, John Heber 40, 83, 94
Hansen, Loretta 79
Hansen, Mary Jane 79
Hansen, Niels 40, 82, 83, 84, 95, 163
Harris, Randy 140
Harvey House 126
Hashknife 162
Hayden, Carl 66
Heber 29, 129, 148
Henning, Ermina 74
Hermit Hermits 69
Highway 260 132
Hog Town 79
Holbrook 2, 19, 33, 37, 40, 43, 65, 72, 79, 89, 102, 120, 126, 129, 130, 148, 164, 165, 168
Holbrook, H.R. 167
Home Depot 163
Hon-Dah 52, 141, *161*, 164
Hon-Dah homesites 132
Horsehead Crossing 167
Horsethief Basin 152
Hudson, Larry 121
Huning, Henry 3, 30, 163

Hunter, Dora 130
Hurricane Lake 164

I

Indian Pine 62
Irwin, B.C. 121

J

Jackson, Anna 77
Jackson Lane 115
Jacques, Sanford 93
Jake Renfro's Famous Log Cabin Cafe 56, 60
javalina 131
Jeffers, Cooney 125
Jennings, James R. 19, 43, 163
John L. Fish Lane 115
Johnny Angel's 141
Johnson, Abe 100
Johnson, Louis E. 83
Johnson, Raymond 100
Johnson Street 115
Jones, Euphie 95
Jones, Glen L. 113
Jones, Sam 94
Jones, Wesley 19
Judson, Maud A. 93
Juniper 8

K

K-Mart 163
Keith, James 40
Kemble, Ron 151
Kinishba Pueblo ruins 165
Kirkland 6

L

La Serrana 127
Lake Mountain Lookout Tower vii

Lakeside viii, 22, 29, 33, 34, 39, 40, 80, 83, 84, 85, 87, 89, 95, 97, 98, 100, 102, 109, 118, 121, 123, 126, 141, 148, 163, 167
Larson, Alof Pratt 82
Larson Memorial Public Library 122
Larson Road 115
Larson, Wallace H. 95
League of Arizona Cities and Towns 121
Lee, Lawrence 101
Lee, Raymond 109
Lee Valley 167
Lee's Drive 115
Lisonbee, Lorenzo 84
Little Bears store 132
Little Colorado River 102, 161, 165
Lone Ranger and Tonto 125
Long, Anthony 162
lookout towers 129
Los Lunas 30
Lotus Garden 141
Lyman Lake 166
Lynch, Richard 2

M

Mack, Walsh 17, 68, 71, 74
Madison, Gray 113
Madison Lane 115
Mal Pai 2
Maricopa County sheriff posse 141
Mason, Joe and Sarah 75, 130
Mason, Sarah 130
McCleve, Aleck 79
McCollough, Joe 162
McCoy Drive 115
McCoy, Sylvester 14, 19
McGuire, Thomas R. 29, 39
McNary vii, 16, 65, 68, 72, 77, 89, 90, 95, 101, 102, 110, 112, 133, 134, 135, 141, 167
McNary, James G. 90, 167
McNeill Street 115
Mead, Norman 2
Mesa Redondo 60

Mectie, Joe 14
Milligan, William 162
Milltown 72, 85
Mogollon prehistoric peoples vi
Mogollon Rim 1, 29, 47, 129
Montano, Patsy 36
Moon Ridge subdivision 115
Morgan, Bill 77
Mormon colonizers 82, 163
Mount Baldy 57
Mount Lemmon 118
mountain lion 131, 164
Mr. C'zs 132
Mullins, Rich 121
Murphy, Nathan 31

N

National Historic Registry 166
Natoli, Jay 121
Navajo, ancestors of vii
Navajo County 4, 95, 100, 119, 123, 130, 161, 163
Navajos 47, 162
Navapache Regional Medical Center 90
Navopache Electric Cooperative 99, 102, 103, 104
Nelson, Willie 69
New Deal's Rural Electrification Administration 99, 102
New York Times 145
Nicklaus, Jack 69
Niels Hansen Drive 115
Nine Pines Motel 5
Noch-ay-del-klinne 44
Northland Pioneer College 129
Nutrioso 167

O

Overacker, Robert 94
Owens, Commodore Perry 163
Owens, James Clark 82

P

Packer, Martha S. 22
Packer, Nephi 4, 36, 40
Palmburg, Blanche 56
Pasta House restaurant 5
Patone 48
Patrol House 127
Paul Bunyan's restaurant 132
Paxon, Debbie 145
Paxon, Jim 144, 145, 150, 151
Pearce, James 165
Pedro 8, 28, 48, 50
Penrod, Albert 8, 82
Penrod, Albert and Mary 14
Penrod, Annie 7
Penrod, Arch 14
Penrod, Cynthia Ann 10, 93
Penrod, Cynthia Jane 33
Penrod, David 7, 10
Penrod, David Israel 34
Penrod, Delbert 8, 12, 28, 31
Penrod, Edna 94
Penrod, Elmer 11
Penrod, Ephraim 8, 11, 40, 79, 93, 135
Penrod, Geneva 8, 10
Penrod, George 15
Penrod, Hattie 94
Penrod, Heber 7
Penrod, Howard 31
Penrod Lane 34, 115
Penrod, Liola 13
Penrod, Liona 8, 10, 13
Penrod, Logan 31
Penrod, Mac 93
Penrod, Marintha A. 22
Penrod, Martin 13, 14, 94
Penrod, Mary Ann 7
Penrod, Mayzetta 36
Penrod, Merry 14
Penrod, Polly Ann 10

Penrod, Ralph 2, 3, 8, 10, 93
Penrod, Reuben "Buster" 135
Penrod, Seid 14
Penrod, Sonny 133, 135
Penrod, Sue 5, 132, 135
Penrod, Thelma Gladys 34
Penrod, William Lewis 2, 3, 7, 8, 10, 22, 28, 31, 33, 34, 40, 94, 109, 135, 136
Penrodville 2
Peterson Drive 115
Peterson, Joseph viii, 82
Phipps Drive 115
Phipps, John William 1, 2, 3, 5, 7, 19, 29, 31, 77, 81, 126, 135
Pinal Apaches 47
Pine 152
Pine Lake 127, 136
pine-bark beetle 151
Pinetop Buffet and Bar-B-Q 74
Pinetop Cemetery 34, 37
Pinetop Cemetery board 136
Pinetop Country Club 112, 113, 115, 140
Pinetop dump 127
Pinetop Elementary School 97
Pinetop Fire Department 123, 134
Pinetop Garden Club 150
Pinetop Hills 112
Pinetop Lakes Golf & Country Club 113
Pinetop Mountain 77, 130, 131, 132
Pinetop Post Office 123
Pinetop Springs 118
Pinetop Water Co. 120
Pinetop-Lakeside 98, 118, 119, 120, 122, 123, 139, 140, 142, 145, 150, 166
Pinetop-Lakeside High School 96
Pinetop-Lakeside Historical Society 100
Pinetop-Lakeside Police Department 140
Pineyon 17
Pollock, Tom 89
Ponderosa Club 64
Ponderosa RV Resort 115
Ponderosa Water Co. 120

Porter Creek 77
Porter, Jim 77
Potter, Pearl 95
Potter, Ruby 95
Prescott 152
Price, Sam 25

Q

Quick, Bill 134
Quick, Grace 134

R

raccoons 131
Rainbow Lake 40, 82, 84, 100, 101, 167
Ramsey, Joe 21
Ranch Wife 125, 129
rattlesnakes 131
Renfro, Ralph Thurston "Jake" 56, 59
Reserve 103
Retzlaff, Wayne 103
Rhoton, Charles 95
Rhoton Lane 115
Rick Fernau 145
Rigney, Walt 3, 19, 81
Rim Road 29, 77, 131, 132
Ringey, Terry 140
Rio Verdes Apaches 47
River Reservoir 165
Rodeo-Chediski fire 104, 118, 130, 134, *139*, 142, 145, 149
Runge, Thelma Wetzel 64

S

Safeway 123
Salt River 47, 164
Salt River Project 164
San Carlos Indian Reservation 43, 47
San Francisco 130
Santa Fe 162
Savage, Charles 4
Sawmill Valley 89

Schuck, Leora Peterson viii, 5, 83, 85
Scorse, Billy 40, 80, 82
Scott, George, James and Robert 77
Scott, Robert 82
Scott's Drive 115
Scott's Reservoir 82
Seavedra, Jose 161
Sells, Dollie 72
Settlers Lane 115
Seven Cities of Gold vii
sheepherders 161
Show Low 2, 3, 4, 29, 30, 40, 77, 82, 84, 121, 129, 139, 141, 142, 148, 161, 162, 163, 168
Shumway, Dick 163
Silver Creek 29, 165
Silver Creek Golf Course 145
Sitgreaves National Forest 103, 112
Smith, Fred 136
Smith, Jessie N. 79
Snow, Erastus 168
Snowflake 82, 127, 161, 165, 168
Southwest Forest Industries 90, 91, 112
Spade, David 69
Springer, Henry 162, 168
Springer Mountain 77
Springerville 66, 71, 103, 161, 162, 163, 166, 168
squirrels 131
St. Johns 161, 167
Stanford University 125, 130
State Route 260 117, 123
Stephens Drive 115
Stephens, William 4, 8
Stewart, John 17
Stinson, James 165
Stock, Joseph 79
Strait, George 69
Stratton, C. B. 40
Sumerhaven 118
Summerhayes, Martha 47
Sunrise Ski Resort 52, 164
Symes 100

T

Taylor 82, 161, 163, 166, 168
Taylor, John 168
The Apache Railway 89
The Arizona Republic 123
The Burly Bear 64
The Lion's Den 74
Tom Mix radio show 125
Tombstone 162, 163
Tontos Apaches 47
Trimble, Marshall 29
Truscott, Lloyd David 36
Tunnel Lake 165
Twomey, Adele 14

U

U.S. Forest Service 94, 103, 112, 129, 148
University of Nottingham in England 125

V

Vasquez de Coronado, Francisco vii
Verde River 164
Victorio 26, 44

W

Wagon Wheel 140
Wakefield, Rhoda P. 43
Wal-Mart 163
Walker, Duane 121
Warm Springs Apaches 47
Warren Ranch 79
water fowl 164
Wayne, John 69, 71
well witcher 113
Wessel, Leslee 122
West, Ezra 93
Wharfield, H.B. 30
White Mountain Apache Tribe 1, 31, 43, 101, 164
White Mountain Apaches 46, 47, 48, 52, 145, 148, 164

White Mountain Country Club 112, 113
White Mountain Electric Cooperative 102
White Mountain Independent 122, 127, 129
White Mountain Indians 47
White Mountain Summer Homes 112
White Mountains vi, 26, 31, 33, 82, 89, 90, 99, 100, 101, 102, 134, 145, 148, 160, 161, 163, 166
White River vii, 101, 164, 168
Whiteriver vii, 34, 79, 91, 98, 101, 140, 149, 168
Wilbur's Market 134
wild turkey 131
Wills, Billy 20
Wills, John 8
Wills, Merrill 40
Willis, Temperance Susan 8
Willson, Roscoe G. 25
Wilson, Belle 62
Wilson, Edith 136
Wilson, Mike 75
Winslow 126
Wise, Tom 64
Woodlake Lake Park 166
Woodland 4, 22, 39, 79, 85, 93, 118, 119, 132
worm races 159

Y

Ye Olde Tavern 159
Young 103
Young, Al 79
Young, Al, Jr. 79
Young, Brigham 30
Young, Polly Ann 7

Z

Zuni 161

About the Author

Gene Luptak and his wife, Dawn, moved to Pinetop in 2001. He worked as a newspaper reporter for over 30 years with *The Arizona Republic* and *The Milwaukee Journal*. He interviewed a man on death row and minutes later watched him die in the gas chamber; he dodged bullets in Prague, Czechoslovakia, during the Russian invasion in 1968; he was part of a crew that flew into the Superstition Mountains to find a dead body. He interviewed such notables as evangelist Billy Graham; comedians George Burns, Jerry Lewis and Milton Berle; lion-tamer Gunther Gebel-Williams; Olympic gold medalists Dorothy Hamill, Mary Lou Retton and Scott Hamilton; and entertainers Phyllis Diller, Pearl Bailey, Perry Como, Tom Jones, Bobby Vinton, Tony Orlando, Tennessee Ernie Ford, Charo and Marie Osmond. Luptak even asked Bob Hope a question once at a press conference. Notwithstanding, an equal thrill came on Oct. 22, 2003, when he caught a 20-inch Rainbow trout that weighed 3 $^1/_2$ pounds at Big Lake. He'd be happy to trade a few Orlandos, Fords and Baileys in for a five-pound cutthroat trout in his beloved adopted home in the White Mountains.

For an extra copy of this book, send $17 (which includes $2 postage, shipping & handling) to: Gene Luptak, c/o Ponderosa Pine Press, P.O. Box 251, Pinetop, AZ 85935. (928) 521-6329. Discount on three or more books. Booksmart@hotmail.com